TEACHING YOUR CHILD TO READ

A STEP-BY-STEP GUIDE TO HELPING YOUR PRESCHOOLER LEARN AND DEVELOP SIMPLE READING SKILLS

JAYNE BEACON

Copyright © 2021 Jayne Beacon. All rights reserved.

The content contained within this book may not be reproduced, duplicated, or transmitted without direct written permission from the author or the publisher.

Under no circumstances will any blame or legal responsibility be held against the publisher, or author, for any damages, reparation, or monetary loss due to the information contained within this book, either directly or indirectly.

Legal Notice:

This book is copyright protected. It is only for personal use. You cannot amend, distribute, sell, use, quote, or paraphrase any part, or the content within this book, without the consent of the author or publisher.

Disclaimer Notice:

Please note the information contained within this document is for educational and entertainment purposes only. All effort has been executed to present accurate, up-to-date, reliable, complete information. No warranties of any kind are declared or implied. Readers acknowledge that the author is not engaged in the rendering of legal, financial, medical, or professional advice. The content within this book has been derived from various sources. Please consult a licensed professional before attempting any techniques outlined in this book.

By reading this document, the reader agrees that under no circumstances is the author responsible for any losses, direct or indirect, that are incurred as a result of the use of the information contained within this document, including, but not limited to, errors, omissions, or inaccuracies.

CONTENTS

Just for you!   7
Introduction   9

PART I
Background Knowledge for You   15

1. THE FOUNDATION: A QUICK GUIDE TO SPEECH AND LANGUAGE DEVELOPMENT   17
   The Standard Milestones of Language Development   18
   What You Can Do to Help   23
   Staying on Top of Problems   25

2. WHAT IS READING AND HOW DO CHILDREN LEARN IT?   27
   So, What Is Reading?   28
   How Do Children Learn to Read?   33

3. PRE-READING: WHAT IS IT AND WHY DOES IT MATTER?   41
   What Is Pre-reading?   41
   Helping Your Child Develop Pre-reading Skills   46

4. RECOGNIZING READING READINESS AND TAKING THE CUE FROM YOUR CHILD   49
   The Four Competencies of Reading Readiness   49
   Signs That Your Child Is Ready to Read   51

PART II
15 Fun Ways to Build Early Reading Skills   55

5. READ, READ, READ! (I'M TALKING TO YOU, MOMMY!) ... 57
   The Vast Benefits of Reading to Children ... 57
   Reading to Babies ... 59
   Reading to Toddlers ... 60
   Reading to Preschoolers ... 61
   Reading to Older Children ... 62
   Tips for Reading to Children ... 62
   Making Reading Part of Your Daily Routine ... 66

6. MAKE STORY TIME INTERACTIVE ... 69
   Key Comprehension Strategies ... 70
   Helping Children to Develop Their Comprehension Strategies ... 73

7. CHATTERBOX: CONVERSATION IS MORE IMPORTANT THAN YOU MIGHT THINK ... 79
   Talking to Little Ones ... 79
   Quality Matters ... 82
   Building Their Skills Through Conversation ... 82

8. PLAYING WITH SOUND, RHYTHM, AND RHYME ... 89
   The Importance of Rhyme, Rhythm, and Repetition ... 89
   Exploring Rhythm and Rhyme with Young Children ... 91

9. BUILDING SEQUENCING SKILLS ... 97
   Helping Children to Develop Sequencing Skills ... 98

10. PRE-WRITING SKILLS (YES, THEY'RE IMPORTANT FOR READING TOO!) ... 103
    What Is Pre-writing? ... 103
    Pre-writing Activities for Preschoolers ... 105
    Transitioning to Writing ... 109
    Making Writing a Natural Part of the Day ... 110

11. A WORLD OF WORDS: RECOGNIZING PRINT IN THE ENVIRONMENT (AND ADDING YOUR OWN!) ... 113
    Environmental Print ... 113

12. IGNITING AN EVERLASTING LOVE OF BOOKS ... 117
    The Search for a Good Book ... 118
    Choosing Books for Different Age Groups ... 119

13. LET'S TELL A STORY: WRITING STORIES TOGETHER ... 125
    Making Up Stories for Your Child ... 125
    Writing Stories Together ... 127

14. LEARNING THE LETTER SOUNDS ... 131
    Understanding the Alphabetic Principle ... 132
    Moving On to Letter Sounds ... 134
    Easy and Fun Ways to Teach the Letter Sounds ... 137

15. HEARING THE SOUNDS IN WORDS ... 143
    Understanding Phonological Awareness ... 143
    Helping Your Child to Hear the Sounds in Words ... 144
    Clues That Your Child Is Struggling ... 146

16. MANIPULATING SOUNDS ... 149
    Strategies for Practicing Phoneme Manipulation ... 149

17. BLENDING AND DECODING WORDS ... 153
    Blending Sounds to Make Simple Words ... 154
    Decoding Words ... 157
    A Step Beyond the Letter Sounds ... 158
    Tips for Teaching Blends, Digraphs, and Trigraphs ... 159

18. THOSE PESKY SIGHT WORDS! ... 163
    The Dolch Sight Words List ... 164
    How to Introduce Sight Words ... 165

19. NOW IT'S THEIR TURN TO READ TO YOU... 169
Tips for Listening to Your Child Read 169

PART III
Going Forward 173

20. THE PARENT PITFALLS YOU CAN EASILY AVOID 175

21. SUPPORTING A LOVE OF READING FROM THIS DAY FORTH 181
Fun Activities for Supporting Reading 182

22. READING GLOSSARY 185

References 197

Just for you

As a way of saying thank you for your purchase, I am offering you an additional very useful companion booklet full of tips and activities to help you understand and kickstart your child's learning journey.

Just scan the QR code below to receive instant access to

8 Essential Development Skills You Need To Teach Your Preschooler.

freeguide.blueyonderpublications.com

INTRODUCTION

"The more that you read, the more things you will know. The more that you learn, the more places you'll go."

— DR. SEUSS, *I CAN READ WITH MY EYES SHUT!*

Some children start kindergarten having heard around 1.4 million more words than their peers. The reason? Those children are read to at home. The children who have the head start have heard five stories a day before they start school. This "million word gap" could be a major explanation for the difference in literacy and vocabulary development in children (Logan et al., 2019).

This certainly correlates with my experience as a teacher's aide. There were always a few children who found it more difficult to get off the ground than others. I remember one child in particular who joined the school in Grade 2 with very few reading skills. I worked closely with her, and I found that what worked best was going back to basics. I used the reading programs my school worked with, of course, but I also drew on what my sister-in-law was doing with her preschoolers—strategies I later went on to use with my own children. The progress this little girl made was staggering. The work we do *before* formal education takes place is so crucial to their eventual success. It allows us to nurture an interest in learning and a love for reading, and if I had ever needed any proof that this was important, this little girl was it.

We only need to look at Finland's education system to see that literacy skills start accumulating before formal education takes place. The Finnish education system is ranked as one of the best in the world, and it differs vastly from the system we have in the States. Children aren't taught to read until the age of seven, but they spend the years before that discovering the joy of learning and picking up the essential creative and problem-solving skills they'll need later. It's true that once they do learn to read, they have a much easier language than English to contend with, but these pre-reading skills and the absence of pressure are also keys to their success.

Believe me, I know your concerns as a parent. I have three kids of my own, and I know the fear that starts to set in as they grow older. How will they get on at school? What if they're not confident enough? What can I do to make sure they have the best school experience possible? We all worry that we're not doing enough, that our children might fall behind or might be held back from reaching their full potential. We want them to love reading for reading's sake, and we want them to see the joy in learning. But with conflicting advice flowing from every corner of the internet, it's all too easy to doubt ourselves.

I've been exactly where you are now. Your little one is developing rapidly, and you're worrying about what you can do to prepare them for education. First, let me tell you that you've got this. There's nothing you need to do that you can't do easily at home.

I'm a stay-at-home mom now. My youngest daughter is four, and I don't plan to return to work until she's a bit older. I've had the privilege of being at home with all of my kids, but I promise you that no matter whether you have a full-time job or the luxury of time with your little ones, you can use every strategy I'll share with you in this book.

By the time we've finished this journey together, you'll know everything you need to do to give your child a head start toward a bright future. You'll be given clear advice on how to prepare your child for reading, and better yet, you'll know how to instill in them a thirst for knowledge. You'll discover everything you need to know to support your child's ongoing education, including vocabulary development, comprehension skills, articulation skills, and perhaps most importantly, an interest in learning. You'll understand how to recognize that your child is ready to read, meeting their natural development patterns, and working at a speed they're comfortable with. You'll be equipped with practical activities you can use with your child to keep them engaged and enthusiastic about reading—without putting them under any pressure.

Maurice Sendak (a firm favorite among all three of my children) said, "You cannot write for children... They're much too complicated. You can only write books that are of interest to them." This perfectly sums up my approach to teaching pre-reading skills. It's not about being rigid and delivering formal lessons: It's about capturing their interest and helping them develop the tools they need to begin their own journey.

This book is the culmination of my years of teaching experience and raising my own children. My kids all love books and learning, and all of them were able to develop the skills they need to get the most out of their education—with very little effort on my part. I'll always remember my eldest, Liam, bowling a waiter over with his reading skills when he was able to read the children's menu and choose what he wanted for lunch. I think he was only about four years old. And then, of course, there's the little girl I told you about earlier. She caught up with her peers by the end of the school year, and you'd never have known she was ever behind.

Everything I'm about to share with you I've tried myself, and my children are living proof that it works. I know how it goes: You're afraid they won't get the education they need in order to reach their potential, and you buy every educational toy under the sun. But let's be honest, the marketing of those toys plays on your fears. That's how companies make their money. You put yourself under enormous pressure, and in the worst cases, children become disillusioned with reading before they've even started. It doesn't have to be this way, and in fact, it shouldn't be. Let's make sure your story has a happier ending.

Before we kick off, let me quickly explain how I've structured this book so you know how to find what you need. Section I will give you the background information you need in order to understand your child's development. In Section II, you'll find tips and activities for building early reading skills. And in Section III, you'll find all the information you need for moving your child forward into the next stage of their learning journey. You won't find the activities in any particular order, but we won't look at anything to do with reading or decoding until the very end of Section II. Don't be alarmed! Remember the Finnish model: There's a lot we need to do before we can introduce them to reading.

So, without further ado… Let's get started!

PART I

BACKGROUND KNOWLEDGE FOR YOU

1

THE FOUNDATION: A QUICK GUIDE TO SPEECH AND LANGUAGE DEVELOPMENT

Every child is unique. They all develop in their own time, and I want you to remember that throughout this chapter. We're going to look at developmental milestones, and it's important that you don't panic if your child doesn't seem to be meeting them. My middle child, Amelia, seemed to meet all the milestones a bit late, and it hasn't impacted her progress at all. Of course, that's not to say that there aren't some instances where a severe delay could be a sign of a deeper problem, and if this is the case, it's always worth consulting a pediatrician.

A basic understanding of language acquisition is helpful for understanding how reading skills are developed, but rest assured that this is a simple introduction and not an in-depth guide. It'll just give you an idea of how your child's language develops, and that'll help you understand what comes later.

THE STANDARD MILESTONES OF LANGUAGE DEVELOPMENT

There are four main components of language: phonology, semantics, grammar, and pragmatics. Phonology has to do with speech sounds and how they're sequenced and structured. Semantics is about meaning and how we express that meaning through words. To illustrate that, let's take the example of anger and rage. The words have a similar meaning, but "rage" implies a stronger feeling or reaction. Semantics is being able to distinguish between these subtleties of language. Grammar, meanwhile, is made up of syntax (word order) and morphology (the structure of words and how they're made up). Pragmatics is about the rules we use for communicating effectively, and it involves using and changing language, and following the rules of effective communication. An everyday example is when we say that we paid for something "with plastic." It's widely accepted that we're specifically referring to a credit or debit card in this context, rather than any other object made from plastic.

Children are wired to develop speech and language from birth, and this process continues throughout childhood, with more complex developments coming later. However, it is most critical during the first five years, when new nerve cells and connections are forming, and stimulation is crucial.

Although children vary in the speed at which they develop speech and language, there is a natural progression throughout the stages. These milestones are useful as a guide to your child's development, and even if they don't reach them at the "right time," they can help you to understand your child's progress.

Standard Speech and Language Milestones

Birth–5 months

- Reacts to loud noises
- Turns head to face sound
- Watches your face when you're talking
- Responds to speech with noise
- Vocalizes pleasure and discomfort (e.g., laughing, giggling, crying)

6–11 months

- Babbling begins (e.g., "ma-ma-ma")
- Understands "No."
- Attempts to communicate through gestures and actions
- Attempts to repeat the sounds you make

12–17 months

- Focuses on a toy or book for around 2 minutes

- Follows simple instructions that are paired with gestures
- Gives non-verbal answers to simple questions
- Points to family members, pictures, and objects
- Attempts to copy simple words
- Labels people or objects with 2 or 3 words (may be unclear)

18–23 months

- Finds pleasure in being read to
- Follows simple instructions (without gestures)
- Points to simple body parts
- Understands simple verbs (e.g., "drink")
- Pronounces most vowels correctly, as well as /h/, /n/, /m/, and /p/
- Beginning to use other speech sounds
- Says 8–10 words (may be unclear)
- Able to ask for common foods
- Makes animal sounds (e.g., "baa")
- Combines words (e.g., "more milk")
- Begins to use pronouns (e.g., "mine")

2–3 years

- Understands around 50 words at 2 years
- Able to say around 40 words at 2 years
- Knows some simple prepositions (e.g., "in")

- Knows pronouns (e.g., "you")
- Knows adjectives (e.g., "big")
- Gaining accuracy of speech (but may leave off end sounds)
- Able to answer simple questions
- Able to use more pronouns
- Speaks in 2 or 3 word phrases
- Uses question inflection (e.g., "My cup?")
- Beginning to use plurals (e.g., "socks")
- Beginning to use regular past tense verbs (e.g., "walked")
- Strangers may be unable to interpret speech

3–4 years

- Able to group objects (e.g., animals, foods)
- Able to identify colors
- Able to use most speech sounds, but may still struggle with more difficult ones
- Uses consonants in words (may not always be accurate)
- Able to describe the use of objects
- Enjoys language (e.g., poems and absurdities)
- Expresses ideas and feelings
- Uses -ing endings on verbs (e.g., "walking")
- Able to answer simple questions
- Able to repeat whole sentences
- Strangers able to interpret most speech

4–5 years

- Understands complex questions
- Understands more complex prepositions (e.g., "behind")
- Speech can be understood but still has difficulty with long or complex words
- Able to say 200–300 words
- Uses some irregular past tense verbs (e.g., "ran")
- Able to describe how to do something
- Able to define words
- Able to list items in a specific category (e.g., animals)
- Able to answer "why" questions

5 years

- Understands over 2,000 words
- Understands time sequences (e.g., "What happened next?")
- Can follow a 3-step instruction
- Understands rhyme
- Engages in conversation
- Can use sentences of 8 words or more
- Uses compound and complex sentences
- Describes objects
- Creates imaginative stories

5–8 years

- Learning more words
- Understands how speech sounds work together
- Becoming better at storytelling
- Able to use different types of sentences
- Shares ideas and opinions
- Able to have adult-like conversations

WHAT YOU CAN DO TO HELP

I can't stress enough that there's nothing you need to formally teach your child to help their language development. These skills develop naturally through the everyday activities you do with your little one: playing, talking, laughing, reading… and what's even better is that these things help their literacy development too. The chances are, you're already doing everything you need to do, and you're doing it naturally. But we all need a little reassurance sometimes, and it could be that there are a few things here you haven't thought of.

Early Years

The best thing you can do for a baby's language development is to talk to them. Respond to their vocalizations. Make gestures, pointing at and naming the things you can both see. Exaggerate your voice when you're describing things, and sing to them whenever you can. Turn everything into a song… Time to go to bed? Sing it. Time to tidy up? Make it into a song. By singing, you're introducing them to rhythm, rhyme, and the natural music within language. You're feeding them new vocabulary constantly, and it's a great opportunity for bonding.

Toddler and Preschooler

Unsurprisingly, talking to your child is still the best thing you can do for them at this age. Instigate conversations about things that have happened recently. Make up stories and get them to help you. I had so much fun with this when my kids were little. It stimulates their language and thinking skills, but it's also great fun and it helps them develop their sense of humor. You can build up the complexity of the vocabulary and grammar you use as they become more secure in their language, and take any opportunity to expand their horizons. When you're reading to them, make it interactive. We'll talk about this a bit more later on, but don't be afraid to get them involved—this is going to do wonders for their literacy skills later.

School Age+

Keep those conversations flowing as your children get older. In our house, we have dinner together as often as possible. Of course, it doesn't always work out that way. If one of them has an activity or my husband's home late, we have to adapt, but it's a good goal to have if you want to build conversation naturally. If you watch a movie, talk about it afterward. Ask them what they think of the books they're reading. Talk about what happened during the day. Talk about anything you like... Just keep talking!

STAYING ON TOP OF PROBLEMS

My goal here is not to make you worry, and I'd like to remind you that timelines and milestones should be taken with a pinch of salt. However, if you feel like there's a delay in their language development, discuss it with your physician. Signs that there may be an issue to address might include a lack of focus or attention, poor eye contact, having difficulty with understanding simple instructions, struggling with social skills, or showing a lack of interest in being read to. If they constantly repeat the same thing or struggle to pronounce words, or if they're only interested in one thing and struggle with imaginative play, it could be a sign that intervention is needed.

Language development paves the way for literacy, and supporting your child through this phase is the first step in helping them to read. The more linguistic input you can give them at this stage, the better, and that really is all you need to do to build a solid foundation for the next phase.

2

WHAT IS READING AND HOW DO CHILDREN LEARN IT?

It seems like a simple question, doesn't it? What is reading? But in order to help your child build up the skills they're going to need to be a confident and fluent reader, it will help you to look at the question a little more closely and understand what exactly it is that reading requires—something a bit beyond your standard dictionary definition.

Before we go further, a word of warning: There are quite a few technical terms that need to be addressed in this chapter. I'll do my best to keep it as engaging as possible, but don't worry: Once we've covered all these bases, we won't need to get so technical again. And rest assured, there's a quick-reference glossary waiting for you in Chapter Twenty-Two to make life easier.

SO, WHAT IS READING?

There are different theories out there about how we learn to read. Some say that reading is a natural process, and that children pick it up on their own as long as they have access to reading material. Others say that reading is made up of strategic context-dependent guess work, and that learning how to do it requires being taught key guessing strategies.

Neither of these theories is true. The reality is that written language is essentially a code, with particular combinations of letters representing certain sounds.

But reading isn't just about decoding and pronouncing those sounds. It also involves reading punctuation and making meaning from the words. It involves understanding vocabulary, and understanding the message of the whole text. Eventually, this will also include making inferences, as well as understanding the meaning clearly written on the page.

Reading is made up of five key skills. These are engaging with books and text, phonemic awareness and phonics skills, fluency, vocabulary skills, and comprehension skills. Let's take a look at what exactly that means in terms of the skills your child is going to need.

Starter Skills

Before any actual reading can occur, your child will need to master a few core skills. This is what you'll be helping them build while you're nurturing their speech and language development. They'll need to have oral language skills in place, and they'll need to understand that the written word is a form of communication. That doesn't mean that they need to understand exactly what this means: They simply need to understand that if they see a word, it means something. In order to make sense of the letters they see, they'll need to be able to distinguish shapes. They'll need to be familiar with how to hold a book, and perhaps most importantly of all, they'll need to have an interest in learning how to read. None of these are skills you need to go out of your way to teach. As long as you're reading to your child, they'll pick them up along the way.

Phonemic Awareness

Phonemic awareness simply means recognizing that the words we say are made up of sounds. It's crucial that a child has this understanding in order to segment and blend the sounds in a word, and from there, decode what that word says. Children need to understand that we produce different sounds by shaping our mouth, lips, and tongue in different ways. They need to be able to blend words when they're given the sounds they're made up of, and segment a given word into its individual sounds. To give you a concrete example, they need to hear the sounds /h/ /a/ and /t/ and blend those sounds to make the word "hat." They also need to be able to hear the word and break it down into its three component sounds. Lastly, they need to be able to identify the initial, medial, and final sounds in a word. So, in our example, they need to be able to tell you that the last sound in "hat" is /t/.

Systematic Phonics

Phonogram List

Vowels					Vowel-Consonants		Consonants			
a	ai	ay	au	aw	augh	er	b	bu	c	ch	ci
e	ea	ee	ew	eigh	cei	ir	ck	d	dge	f	g
ei	ey	i	ie	igh	ed	ear	gn	gu	h	j	k
o	oa	oe	oi	oy	ough	ear	kn	l	m	n	ng
oo	ou	ow	u	ui		ar	p	ph	qu	r	s
						or	sh	si	t	tch	th
						wor	ti	v	w	wh	wr
							x	y	z		

Systematic phonics is the written code we use to represent a sound as a visual image. Unfortunately, that's a pretty complex code in the English language. We have 44 speech sounds, and 75 phonograms (the groups of characters we use to represent them). Some of these have one letter, such as "h." Some have two, like "ai" or "oy." Others have three (e.g., "igh") or four (e.g., "ough"). And as if that wasn't complicated enough, some phonograms make more than one sound—think of the phonogram "ou" as it sounds in "house," "four," "you" and "cousin," for example. And on top of all that, there are 31 spelling rules that dictate how different spellings are used in English.

Fluency

Fluency requires your child to master both phonemic awareness and systematic phonics to a level at which they become automatic. This is developed through using these skills and practicing regularly, eventually reaching automaticity. When you watch a proficient reader read whole words, what they're actually doing is decoding the individual sound in those words at such a pace that it appears to be instant. Until a child has a certain level of fluency, they'll find it more difficult to make meaning out of what they're reading because the brain needs to focus too much on decoding to have much room left for higher-order thinking skills.

Vocabulary Skills

As your child's language develops, they learn the meaning of new words and morphemes, eventually understanding that new words often contain clues about their meaning. A morpheme is a unit of meaning within a word. Let's take the word "undefeatable" as an example. The morphemes here are "un," "defeat," and "able." Each of them provides a clue as to the meaning of the word. Most of the words in the English language contain a Latin root, so understanding the meaning of the most common ones helps with comprehension. As your child's reading develops, they'll acquire more and more vocabulary, and they'll be able to work out the meaning of unfamiliar words by looking at the context and the morphemes within each word.

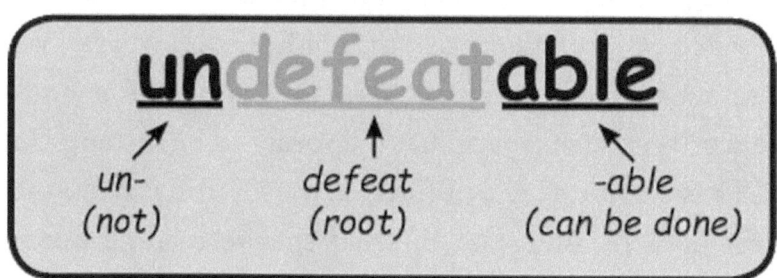

Comprehension Skills

These are the skills that children need in order to understand a whole text. They develop gradually as children gain the foundational skills of reading. They start by understanding single words, then phrases, followed by short sentences, paragraphs, and in the end, whole books. As their ability grows, they'll build skills like being able to recall information, identify important details, summarize what they've read, make predictions, make inferences, and form their own opinion on the text.

Bringing It All Together

All of these foundational skills need to be in place in order for a child to become a fluent and confident reader.

This brings us neatly to Scarborough's Reading Rope, a clear infographic created by the early language development and literacy researcher Hollis Scarborough.

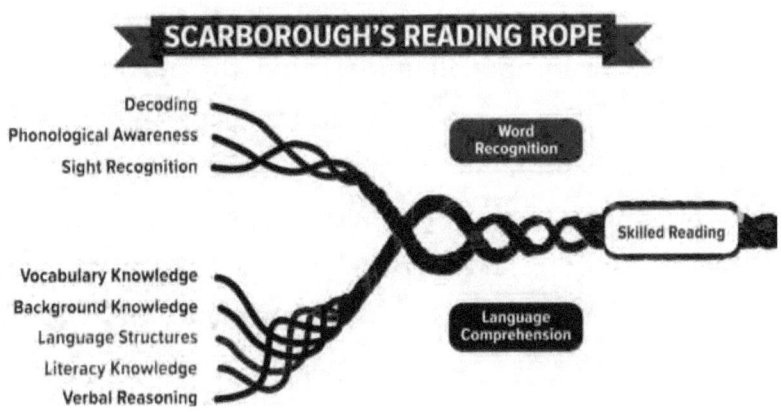

As you can see, the rope is made up of upper and lower strands. The word-recognition strands intertwine as the reader acquires accuracy and fluency, while the language-comprehension strands intertwine and meet the word-recognition skills, resulting in a proficient reader. This process takes time and practice.

HOW DO CHILDREN LEARN TO READ?

First off, let's just remind ourselves that children are different, and they won't all learn in exactly the same way. However, we can use a generalization to get an idea of the process.

It starts with emerging literacy. This is the gradual process of using and understanding language, starting with speaking and listening, and moving through to reading and writing. This is what you'll see before your child starts school. From there, they'll build on their early skills. By the end of kindergarten, most children will understand that print contains meaning. They'll recognize written language, and they'll be able to identify and name the letters of the alphabet. They'll know that these letters are linked to sounds, and they'll know what sound each letter makes. They'll also know that words can be used for different reasons, and they'll understand how books work to convey meaning.

By the end of the second grade, they'll be working on their comprehension skills through reading a range of texts, and they'll be able to analyze words as they're reading. They'll understand the main elements of stories, such as the setting and the characters, and they'll recognize some of the characteristics of certain genres (for example, distinguishing between a poem and a funny story).

Reading Milestones

Just as we saw with speech and language development, these milestones are a guideline. Remember that children don't all develop at the same rate, and some children may not quite hit the milestones "on time." My daughter Amelia fits into this bracket, and she's proven time and time again that she gets there in the end.

Standard Reading Milestones

Birth–12 months

- Starts reaching for soft or board books
- Shows an interest in the pictures in books
- Responds to a story with sound
- Helps to turn the pages in a book

1–2 years

- Engages with pictures and names familiar concepts
- Answers questions about the pictures
- Recognizes their favorite books from the covers
- Recites words from their favorite stories
- Pretends to read by making up stories and turning the pages

3–4 years

- Understands how to hold a book
- Understands that text is read left-to-right from the top of the page
- Notices rhyming words
- Starts retelling stories
- Recognizes roughly 50% of the alphabet
- Begins matching sounds with letters
- Recognizes their name and other familiar words in print

5 years

- Can match letters to sounds
- Can identify initial, medial, and final sounds in spoken words
- Can create new words by changing the initial sound
- Can match the words they hear to printed words
- Recognizes some words by sight
- Gaining accuracy of speech (but may leave off end sounds)
- Asks different types of questions about a story
- Can retell a story in sequence
- Can predict what will happen next in a book
- Starts reading or asking to hear stories for fun
- Uses story language during conversation or play

6–7 years

- Learning rules of spelling
- Increased recognition of words by sight
- Improvements in fluency and speed of reading
- Uses context to understand new words
- Rereads something that doesn't make sense
- Connects reading material to personal experience

8–10 years

- Makes the transition from learning to read to reading in order to learn
- Able to read multisyllabic words
- Learning about root words, prefixes, and suffixes
- Reading for different reasons
- Can describe the main components of a story
- Can summarize the sequence of events in a book
- Can identify themes in stories
- Can make inferences from the text
- Can compare information across texts
- Can refer to the text when questioned on it
- Understands figurative language

Middle school and high school

- Continuing to expand vocabulary and reading more complex material
- Can analyze character development and plot devices
- Can identify themes and analyze their development
- Able to support their analysis with textual evidence
- Can analyze ideas in the text
- Understands more complex linguistic devices

The Main Approaches to Teaching Reading

There are three ways that reading can be taught. The first is phonics-based teaching, in which spelling rules are introduced and children are taught to use their phonetic knowledge to decode the words they read. The second is the "whole language" approach, and this method requires children to recognize words as complete units of language. With this method, words are not decoded according to their letters; rather the whole word is learned in relation to its meaning. This is a rare approach these days, and those who use it tend to use "embedded phonics" alongside it, where children are taught to understand the relationship between letters and sounds as they read. This is often referred to as the "hybrid approach," and gives us our final strategy.

Personally, I prefer the phonics-based approach, but I think we can learn something from the whole language approach too. With phonics-based teaching, children learn the skills they need to decode almost any word, whereas with the whole language approach, they know only the words they have learned. When they come upon a new word, they're forced to guess, and too much guessing means that they can't understand what they're reading. Eventually, this will lead to a dip in self-esteem, and learning progress will halt.

There are some words, however, where sounding out a word simply won't work. Take the word "one," for example. If children blend the sounds /o/ /n/ /e/, they won't arrive at the correct word. Words like this are best taught as "sight words," which we'll look at in Chapter Eighteen, and this is where we can borrow from the whole language approach.

In my opinion, early learners have the most success with a largely phonics-based approach, and this is the angle I'll be taking throughout the book. But before we even get to building phonological awareness, we need to start with nurturing our children's pre-reading skills.

3

PRE-READING: WHAT IS IT AND WHY DOES IT MATTER?

So, we've looked at how children learn to read, but this process begins long before they meet their teacher. It all starts with their emerging literacy skills, or pre-reading.

WHAT IS PRE-READING?

It is your child's pre-reading skills that will set them up to decode words and understand what they're reading, and these must be developed before they can begin to read. These can be boiled down to five key skills.

Print Awareness

This requires a child to understand that letters come together to make words which have specific meanings. In a book, those words come together to tell a whole story or a particular message. Children must also understand that words must be read in a particular order, with people reading from left to right on the page, and from the start of the book to the end of it.

Motivation to Read

Before a child can learn to read, they need the desire to understand what's in a book. This develops naturally as children develop print awareness and listen to stories being read to them. A child isn't ready to learn until they have this skill in place, and trying to force it too soon won't help them.

Listening Comprehension

I make a distinction here between listening comprehension and reading comprehension because even before a child reads for meaning, they need to understand the stories they hear. You'll know your child has this skill when they're able to answer your questions about a story, ask their own, or summarize what they've just heard. These are the skills they'll build on later when they're reading themselves.

Letter Knowledge

In order to progress to blending sounds and decoding words, children need to understand the difference between lowercase and uppercase letters, and recognize the letters of the alphabet and the sounds they make. This is letter knowledge.

Phonological Awareness

Phonological awareness is a phrase you'll probably hear quite a lot once your child starts school, but it begins before they even start to read. It refers to hearing the distinct sounds words are made up of: the sounds at the beginnings and ends of words; the sounds in the middle; and the rhyming patterns linking words together. Once this is in place, children will have the skills they need to blend, decode, and manipulate sounds.

Pre-reading Behaviors to Watch Out For

These skills make up the foundation of emerging literacy we discussed in the last chapter. There are a few behaviors you'll see more often as they begin to consolidate these skills.

These are the behaviors that start to emerge from a young age before any formal teaching has taken place (*see Table 1*).

Building on Early Skills

Once your child goes to school and begins to flourish as a reader, they'll build on the emerging skills you saw developing at home. Here's what this may look like (*see Table 2*).

Behavior	Relation to Literacy
Creating a pattern out of objects (e.g., beads)	They're building an understanding of sequencing, which will help them understand that words are read in a particular order.
Talking about a story after listening to it	Through this process, children learn that books contain ideas, people, and places, and as they listen to stories and talk about them, they're building their vocabulary.
Playing matching games	Matching games require children to see that some things are identical, and this helps form the foundation they'll need to understand that the letters in a word have to be written in the same order each time in order to have meaning.
Following directions to move along to music	This will give them an understanding of concepts of direction and enable them to add these words to their vocabulary. Eventually, this will lead to their understanding of how the words on a page are read.
Reciting poems and making up their own rhymes	During this process, children become aware of phonemes, and they will build on this understanding as they begin to read and write.
Making signs for a make-believe shop	Here, they are practicing using the written word to provide information.
Retelling a story to a soft toy or another child	This behavior is a sign of their growing confidence in their ability to learn how to read. They are practicing telling a story in the right order.
Making a grocery list using invented spelling	Here, they are using words to share information. While their spelling may be invented, it encourages them to build phonemic awareness.
Signing their name on a painting or attendance chart	They are beginning to understand that their names represent them, and that other objects are represented by other words. They are beginning to understand that writing has a purpose.

Table 1. *Pre-reading Behaviors to Watch Out For*

Behavior	Relation to Literacy
Discussing the rules for a class trip while their teacher creates a written list	Here, children are learning how speaking, listening, reading, and writing are connected. Language is being used for a purpose.
Looking for information in a book	This shows that children understand that print holds information, and they know that they can use books as a resource for finding it.
Independently reading a book they've heard read to the class	Children are reading for fun, and they can use the words they remember hearing to help them work out the rest. They can do this because they remember the order of the story and its meaning.
Reading some words without needing to sound them out	They are building up a sight vocabulary that includes the most frequently used words, which they can now read automatically.
Reading unfamiliar words	Here, children are using what they know to work out new words, consolidating their skills each time.
Using new words in speech and writing	Through talking, listening, reading, and exploring their interests, children are building their vocabulary, and understanding its meaning as they begin to use it.
Recognizing spelling mistakes and asking for help to rectify them	As well as learning basic spelling rules and their exceptions, they understand that spelling requires more than just matching letters and sounds.
Asking questions about the books they read	They understand that reading means more than pronouncing the words on the page, and ask questions for clarification or to learn more.
Choosing to read in their own time	They are working to become better readers, enjoying reading independently and taking ownership of the books they choose.

*Table 2. **Building on Early Skills***

HELPING YOUR CHILD DEVELOP PRE-READING SKILLS

We'll look at this in much more detail in Section II, but it will be helpful for you to go in with some general knowledge of how to build pre-reading skills through language. What I love about this is that it's almost hard *not* to help children develop.

The single most important thing you can do for them is talk to them. The more you talk to your child, the more vocabulary they will hear, and the more advanced their language use will become. Everything is an opportunity for a chat with your little one: at the park; in the car; at bathtime… Use every chance you get, and be guided by your child. They're exploring their own interests every day, so follow those interests and talk about them. If they point to an object and give you that quizzical look, translate their pointing into words: "Yes, that's a dog. Look at him wagging his tail."

Introduce your child to new words at every opportunity. Let's take snack time for example. Those cucumber slices are many things: tasty, delicious, crunchy, yummy, healthy, green, round… It doesn't matter if you're using words they don't yet understand. It is this process that will help them understand them. Narrate what both you and your child are doing: "Let's wipe up the crumbs now," or "You're making all that cucumber disappear!"

As your child begins to speak for themselves, they'll make mistakes. They'll get the words wrong, and they'll mispronounce things. You don't need to correct them when this happens. All you need to do is let them hear the correct pronunciation. For example, perhaps your child says "Pasgetti." Rather than correcting their mistake, you can say something like, "Would you like more spaghetti? It's tasty, isn't it?" This gives them a chance to hear how the word should sound without putting them off trying new words for fear of getting them wrong. Avoid the temptation to speak for your child too. You'll probably find that they'll go through a stage where you can understand them, but other adults can't. What you can do in this situation is translate for them afterward, but let them have their chance to speak first.

You've probably been doing a lot of this work already. Every time you talk to your little one—or sing, or read to them—you're laying another block in their foundations.

4

RECOGNIZING READING READINESS AND TAKING THE CUE FROM YOUR CHILD

The strategies we'll be looking at in the next section are focused on building reading skills to the point where a child is ready to read. Pushing them too hard too soon will put your child under unnecessary pressure, and you won't get the results you're hoping for—even if they've theoretically reached the age they should have hit a particular milestone. In this chapter, we'll take a look at the signs that your child is ready to read so that you recognize them when they appear.

THE FOUR COMPETENCIES OF READING READINESS

A common mistake made by both parents and teachers is believing that once a child knows the letter sounds and names, they're ready to read, but the reality is much more complex than this. They need to have four key competencies in place before they're truly ready to read.

The first of these is **social development**. This is important because in order to read, children need to have developed a certain level of self-control and understand how to take turns and cooperate. A lot of the teaching involved in reading development will involve discussion and activities, and your child won't be able to access these without these social skills in place.

The second competency they'll need is **emotional development**, which is necessary in order for them to understand how they fit into the world. On top of this, they need **physical development**. Their body needs to be strong enough to support sitting in order to read, and they need fine motor skills in order to turn the pages and begin writing.

Lastly, they will need their **cognitive development** to have reached a certain level. They need to be able to discriminate between the shapes and sounds of the letters, which requires both visual and auditory discrimination skills. This means they will need to be able to see the similarities and differences between the letters, and they'll need to be able to hear the difference between similar sounds (like /f/ and /v/).

SIGNS THAT YOUR CHILD IS READY TO READ

To make these a bit easier to spot, I've split them into two broad categories: physical signs and language signs. They're not in any particular order, and your child may develop some much more quickly than others. Remember that all children develop at slightly different paces, so there's no need for concern if one of their friends shows some of these signs earlier. When the majority of these skills are in place, you'll know that the four key competencies have been met and your child is ready to learn how to read.

Physical Signs

Crossing the midline: Younger children will switch hands in front of their body while they're trying to grasp an item from their opposite side. Once they are able to hold something in one hand and bring it across the front of their body, their brain is able to shift an item from right to left or vice versa: an important skill if they're to follow words across a page.

Following an object with their eyes: If you hold a toy level with your child's nose and move it across their line of sight, can their eyes follow it smoothly? If their eyes jump when you cross the midline, they're not yet ready to read, as they'll have trouble tracking words.

Skipping using opposite sides of the body: This one may come a little later. If your child is able to swing one arm at the same time as hopping on the opposite foot, their body has a physical connection between the two sides of the body. For children who live with a disability, or for any other reason are unable to skip, you can see the same signal by playing clapping games. If they are able to clap their hands and then clap a partner's hands in a rhythmic pattern, this is a good sign that both sides of the brain are working together.

Standing on one leg with their eyes either open or closed: If your child still struggles to stand on one leg (and they are physically able), they are still developing the brain-body connection they're going to need in order to read. If they're able to keep their eyes closed while they're balancing, they have a good sense of their body's position in space, even in the absence of visual signs. If they still need those signs, they're not yet ready to focus on reading.

Drawing themselves: When your child is able to draw themselves (with at least ten parts of the body included), it shows you not only that they know their own body, but that they can translate it onto paper. This shows that their brain is ready to understand the differences between the letters.

Language Signs

Showing an interest in books and words: In order to learn to read themselves, children need to be interested in the books you read to them. They should be interested in the pictures and turning the pages, and they should know how to handle a book (i.e., that it must be a particular way up and read in a particular order).

Playing word games and rhyming: Once a child is able to hear the final sounds in words and can make rhymes out of them, they're showing you that they understand the idea of phonemes. If they can't yet hear how two words sound similar, they'll struggle to look for letter patterns shared between words, and this will make reading difficult.

Identifying shapes and using prepositions to describe their positions: In order to understand the difference between letters, children will need to recognize the difference between sizes and shapes. If you draw them a triangle and a circle, can they tell you which shape is above the other? If you draw two squares, can they tell you which one is bigger?

Identifying letters: Your child will need to be able to identify the majority of the letters of the alphabet by either their sound or their name. I can't recommend alphabet fridge magnets enough for helping them with this.

Reading their name and showing an interest in other words: Their own name is the first word most children are able to read. If you write theirs down with a few words alongside it, do they ask you what the other words say? This shows that they understand that these words have meaning, and they want to know what that meaning is.

The activities and skills we're going to look at now don't assume reading readiness. Rather, they will help your child to get there, and give them a strong foundation to leap off from when they do begin to read in earnest. We'll end each of the next fifteen chapters with a simple game you can play with your child to help them build their literacy skills. They won't all directly relate to the skill discussed in the chapter, but remember that no single skill is developed in a vacuum. Remember Scarborough's Reading Rope: All the skills come together to form the complete skill of reading.

PART II

15 FUN WAYS TO BUILD EARLY READING SKILLS

5

READ, READ, READ! (I'M TALKING TO YOU, MOMMY!)

I can't emphasize enough the importance of reading to your child. It has benefits that extend even beyond literacy development. Let's start with these so we get a good idea of the complete picture.

THE VAST BENEFITS OF READING TO CHILDREN

First and foremost, reading is an opportunity for you to bond with your child. Research has shown that reading together fosters a strong parent-child relationship (Duursma, Augustyn, and Zuckerman, 2008). Being read to gives children a sense of security, and sharing a positive experience of a book with an adult helps them to view reading in a positive light. It also nurtures their listening skills, which is important if they are to read for themselves.

When children listen to a story, their vocabularies are expanding, and they're acquiring words they may not hear in everyday conversation. We already mentioned the "million word gap"... This is why! This works for babies too. Even though they may seem too young to understand the words they're hearing, babies who are exposed to a lot of language score higher on cognitive development and language tests, and this continues well into their teen years (Mendelsohn and Klass, 2018).

Their creativity benefits too. Stories expose your child to whole new worlds, and non-fiction books feed them with new information. I don't need to tell you how vivid a child's imagination can be, and reading only furthers this. Creativity helps children to develop their ideas and explore their interests, and it's good for their emotional wellbeing too.

Despite this boost in creativity, listening to a story also helps to develop a child's attention span. As you continue to read to your child, you'll notice that over time, that squirmy, distracted toddler becomes a fully attentive listener. Throughout this process, they're developing a longer attention span and building their retention skills.

Reading also gives your child the opportunity to learn how to cope with stressful experiences before they happen in real life. Reading stories about a difficult situation (starting a new school, for example), gives your child a chance to familiarize themselves with the feelings they might experience, and gives you the opportunity to talk through what might be worrying them. This is useful for non-stressful situations too: Books have the power to show them what happens in a whole range of situations, giving them a reference point for when they experience them themselves.

READING TO BABIES

You're never too young to be read to. Even babies under six months can benefit from books with simple, bright pictures —just make sure there's a lot of contrast on the page. Books at this age don't need to have words, but you can (and should) talk to your baby as you're going through them, varying your tone and making your voice musical to keep them engaged. They will also benefit from hearing lullabies and nursery rhymes at this age: It's all language exposure, and it's all introducing them to the rhythm and rhyme of language, which, as you'll see in Chapter Eight, is important to their literacy development.

As they get a bit older, you can progress to books with simple text that relates to the picture, ideally with lots of rhythm. By the time your child is between twelve and eighteen months, they might enjoy books that show children doing ordinary things, or books with animals and familiar characters in them. At this stage, pictures can be more detailed, and a simple story will be appropriate. Once they're babbling, you can even get them involved in talking about the pictures, using questions like, "What's that?" or "Can you see the monkey?" Stay positive, and repeat any misconceptions back to them with the correction modeled at the end. For example, you might say something like, "Yes, he looks like a dog, doesn't he? But he's actually a fox."

Babies, as I'm sure you know, are very hands-on, so look for sturdy board, vinyl, or fabric books. Many baby books also have valuable sensory experiences built into them, so look out for fun additions like crinkly pads and furry characters.

When you're reading to your baby, you want to aim for brief but frequent sessions, aiming to read often every day.

READING TO TODDLERS

Children between nineteen and thirty months (approximately—remember there are no rules here) usually engage well with books that contain familiar characters. They want to see pictures, action, and details rather than a lot of words on the page. Short stories that involve causal relationships or problems for characters to solve usually work well. You'll also want to look for books that involve repetition: books involving song, rhyme, or other modes of repetition. If you pause when you're reading books like this, your little one may well start to fill in the blank with a repeated word.

Continue to talk around the stories, making connections between the book and your child's experiences. You might say something like, "She's eating all her dinner, just like you do," or "That dog looks a bit like Fluffy, doesn't he?"

Once children have reached this stage, durability is a little less important, and you can graduate to books with paper pages. Be aware that they may still rip the pages, though, so you'll probably want to supervise them when they're handling the book by themselves.

READING TO PRESCHOOLERS

There's a huge diversity in children's abilities at this stage, so the best advice I can give you is to let them take the lead when you're choosing the complexity of a book. Preschoolers will still enjoy pictures with little in the way of text, but once they reach school age, some may be able to deal with more complex plots that involve more words than pictures. As they begin to read themselves, you can involve them in the story by asking them to read a few words. I'd recommend only doing this with familiar books, however; otherwise you run the risk of interrupting the story and making the process less fun for them. At this age, it's crucial that reading doesn't become a chore. If you want them to love reading and have the drive to learn, you want them to be excited by the reading experience.

No matter how simple or complex the book is, what you can certainly do is ask questions as you go along. This both allows you to check their comprehension, and encourages them to build on it. Aim for open-ended questions like, "What might happen next?" to encourage them to look beyond the surface.

Daily reading is important, but preschoolers will also benefit from extra literacy activities like reading cereal boxes, listening to audiobooks, and singing songs. These activities are all good for their literacy development.

READING TO OLDER CHILDREN

It can be tempting to think that once children can read for themselves, there's no longer any need to read to them. But reading to your child is always beneficial—even up until their early teens. It's still good for their emotional development, and it's still good for their academic progress. Personally, I find it's also just such a lovely time to share with them. My eldest son is ten now, and he has so many activities going on that this quiet time with him is a precious luxury. At his age, it's mostly about fluency and comprehension, so we always talk about the book, and I always ask questions to check that he understands more complex ideas.

TIPS FOR READING TO CHILDREN

Before we go on with this section, a quick caveat: The most important thing is that you read to your child. Overanalyzing it to the point that you feel insecure won't help you, and it won't help them. I've put together these tips to give you ideas and help you out, but you shouldn't use them as boxes you have to tick. Any reading you do is valuable, no matter how you do it. However, here are a few nuggets of advice to help you make the experience as fun and enriching as possible for both you and your child.

Be consistent: Aim to make reading to your child part of your daily routine (we'll talk about this more a little further down the chapter). For many people, this means having a regular slot that their children know they can look forward to, but at the very least, aim to fit it into the day at some point. If your child asks you, "Is it story time yet?" you know you're doing something right.

Give it your full attention: It doesn't have to be a long story, but it does have to be a complete experience, and that means you need to be fully present. If you want to make the most of that bonding time with your child and encourage them to love reading, the phone will have to be set aside, and the dishes will have to be left for later.

Choose a book you both enjoy: This is perhaps a little more difficult when they're very young, but as they get older, try to look for books that you'll both enjoy. Even very young children can enjoy chapter books if you make them engaging and their attention span is up to it. If you enjoy the story as much as your child does, it'll make it easier to be fully present in the moment and make the story engaging and interactive.

Engage with the story: While I do encourage asking questions and talking about the book, as you'll see in a moment, be careful not to overuse these tactics. Children won't enjoy the story as much if you stop every few minutes to check their comprehension. Try to save this for the beginnings and ends of your sessions, and focus on experiencing the story together while you're reading.

Relax about your style: While character voices and rich expression are great, not everyone is comfortable with doing this. My own mother is dyslexic, and she has never been a confident reader, yet I still look back on story time with her with fondness. Your children aren't judging your performance. They're just enjoying being in this moment with you and being transported into another world.

Re-read the favorites: Most young children go through a phase where they want to hear the same story over and over again. While it's important that you're interested and engaged in the reading experience, I'd recommend balancing this with reading other books rather than refusing to read *that* story again. That book is capturing their interest, and maybe even fulfilling an emotional need, so if they want to carry on reading it, keep it in the mix.

Help them see the joy of reading: Your ultimate goal is to encourage a love of reading in your child, and that means reading great stories that captivate their interests. Aim to read lots of different books that introduce them to a range of different ideas and themes.

Ask questions: While I think it's important not to interrupt the flow of the story with constant questions, it *is* a good idea to check your child's comprehension every now and then. With little ones, questioning is easier to do more frequently: "Where's the dog?" or "Can you see the ball?" As they get older, you can ask questions like, "What do you think might happen next?" or "How would you feel if that happened to you?" Once you're reading chapter books with them and the story continues over a couple of nights, you can use your questions to recap on the previous night's reading or finish up at the end of the session: "Can you remember what happened in the last chapter?" or "What do you think will happen when the characters get to the zoo?"

Encourage little ones to act out the story: A good tip for getting younger children engaged in the story is to make it active. Perhaps they can show you how tall the giraffe is with their arms, or demonstrate that they can hop like a bunny too.

Talk about the book: Again, for younger children, sometimes talking about the pictures in the book is more valuable than reading the words on the page. Perhaps the words say, "The dog is running," but there's much more to say than this: "Look at how fast he's going! He's going home for his lunch —just like you do after preschool. We're going to have lunch soon." What you're doing here is relating the world of the book to their own experiences, developing their vocabulary, and engaging their interest at the same time.

Give them ownership of reading: Even little children can help you "read" the book. Let them hold it. Let them turn the pages and touch the pictures. Children need to know that reading is an interactive experience that they can be involved in, and planting this seed early on will help to motivate them to read for themselves later.

MAKING READING PART OF YOUR DAILY ROUTINE

Many parents find that bedtime is the easiest way to integrate reading into their daily routine, and I have to say, this is how it's usually been in my house. This doesn't work for everyone though: Perhaps your child is too cranky before bed, or perhaps you're too tired yourself. The most important thing is to find something that works for you and your child. Here are a few ideas if you're struggling with that.

- Five minutes at the start of the day before they get up
- Bathtime
- While they're eating breakfast
- In the car or on the subway
- When you drop them off at daycare
- In waiting rooms
- At nap time

One thing I'd like to add to all of this is that you're a role model for your children. I still remember my parents reading in the evening and looking forward to reading on vacation (my mom may have been dyslexic, but she still loved reading), and this was powerful. It made reading an important part of my life from a very young age. If your children see you reading, they'll see that it's something that has value, and as they grow older, they'll have an interest in learning the skills they need to access the books you love. I always make time for my own reading now, and I make sure my children see me doing this.

Nearly every resource you come across about developing your child's literacy skills will mention the importance of reading to them. This is something you want to build into daily life. From my own personal experience, I'd recommend including it as part of your child's bedtime routine, which tends to be vulnerable to less compromise than other parts of the day, but do what works for you and your family. There's no right or wrong way to go about it.

★ Game Time!

I Spy is a great game for developing your child's pre-reading skills. You can vary the game so that objects must be spied by their initial sounds ("I spy with my little eye, something beginning with /s/.") or by their color ("I spy with my little eye, something the color red." Best of all, this game can occupy children for hours, and they have no idea they're learning at the same time.

6

MAKE STORY TIME INTERACTIVE

Reading to your child, especially when they're very young, is a naturally interactive experience, but there are things you can do to enhance their comprehension skills and vocabulary acquisition as you go.

Discussing what you're reading and asking questions is all you need to do to nurture comprehension skills and make reading an interactive experience. Young children will also ask you questions—when they're given the space to do so, they'll naturally build on their skills.

Before we get into what you can do to help them, let's take a look at the comprehension skills they're working toward.

KEY COMPREHENSION STRATEGIES

Using Background Knowledge

The background knowledge we bring to reading is made up of our experiences and our understanding of how written language works. This knowledge is crucial if we are to understand what we're reading. There's a phenomenon in psychology known as schema theory, which says that as we learn about the world, we build up a network of structures (schemas) which interconnect. These structures grow and develop as we learn new information, either from our experiences or from reading.

Let's take the example of a cat. The schema a young child has for a cat might only contain their understanding of their pet cat. But as they acquire more experiences and meet different cats in different settings, their schema for a cat will grow and connect to other schemas (such as those relating to vets or varieties of cat).

So, what does this mean for reading comprehension? Good readers are able to connect their background knowledge (both of the world and of their understanding of text organization) to the information they find in the text, activating existing schemas immediately. This has a knock-on effect on other schemas, enabling them to understand what they're reading.

Asking Questions

This involves us asking ourselves questions as we read, which enables us to integrate information, summarize what we've read, and identify the main points. When we're able to ask the right questions, we can zone in on the most important information in the text and tackle any problems we have with our understanding.

Making Inferences

When we make inferences, we're drawing conclusions from what we're reading when there may not be an explicit explanation. Essentially, we're "reading between the lines" by combining the words on the page with our background knowledge. When we show children how to make inferences, they are better equipped to make meaning from a text, which is essential to good reading.

Making Predictions

Our ability to make predictions as we read helps us connect our prior knowledge to new information in order to understand what we're reading. For example, when we pick up a book, we might use what we already know about the author to predict what that book will be about. When we read a headline, memories of articles with similar content are triggered, allowing us to predict the sort of information we're likely to find in the article. We make predictions constantly as we read, often subconsciously, and we evaluate and update them as we go. This is a skill that helps us to understand and contextualize the new information we encounter.

Summarizing

Summarizing a text allows us to bring together all the information and explain it in our own words. It's what allows us to recall what we've read quickly, and identify what's important and how different pieces of information relate. This is equally as important when we read a fiction piece as it is when we read a non-fiction text.

Visualizing

As we read, we make mental images in order to understand what we're reading. This is particularly useful in a narrative text, when we can visualize the characters or the setting, but it's also helpful when we're reading non-fiction pieces, allowing us to form an image to help us understand a particular concept.

Comprehension Monitoring

The final piece in the comprehension puzzle is the ability to recognize when we don't understand what we've read and take steps to rectify this. This might include rereading the text, reading ahead, or looking up an unfamiliar word.

Proficient readers are able to use the full range of comprehension strategies, sometimes filtering out the ones that are less useful to them. They have conscious control of these strategies, and can choose when to use them. This is what we're aiming to develop in our children.

HELPING CHILDREN TO DEVELOP THEIR COMPREHENSION STRATEGIES

Becoming an active reader is the key to developing solid comprehension strategies, and this is what you're nurturing in the pre-reading stage. As your child gets older, you can help them develop these strategies so they can make meaning from what they read. What's great about this is that it's very easy to do, but has a huge impact on their reading development.

Making connections: By helping your child to make connections between what they're reading (or being read) and their existing knowledge, you're helping them to understand how their background knowledge relates to their understanding. You can help them make connections by talking about shared memories that relate to what you're reading, or similar situations you know they're familiar with. Over time, your child will begin to make these connections themselves.

Asking questions: We've discussed the importance of questioning quite a lot already. It encourages your child to look for clues in the book and make predictions and inferences.

Making "mind movies": You can help your child become aware of visualization and begin to use it independently by describing what scenes look like when you're reading. For example, if a scene takes place on the beach, you can describe the image you see, the smell of the ocean, and the way you feel calm and happy. Invite your child to do the same, and talk about what's similar and what's different about your mind movies. You can even take this a step further by asking your child to draw a picture of the scene.

Looking for clues: Helping your child to find clues in the text will help them to make predictions and inferences. If a character on the front of a book has wet hair and is wearing a swimsuit, ask your child what they could have been doing. What do they think the book might be about? Encourage your child to look for clues in the words too: If a character yawns, what does this tell you about how they're feeling?

Discussing what's important: Helping your child to identify the most important information will also help their comprehension skills. Ask them who the main characters are and what problem they're facing. Ask them what's happened in the story so far. These questions encourage them to summarize and ask their own questions in order to make meaning from what they're reading.

Although some comprehension strategies (inference, for example) are higher-level skills, all of them can be nurtured at any age. It's simply a case of adapting your questioning to suit their level of understanding. Below you'll find some quick ideas and questions you can use to help your children, whatever developmental stage they're at. These are just examples, however: Any question you ask is valuable.

Making Reading Interactive for Babies and Toddlers

- Show them the cover page
- Let them turn the pages
- Talk/sing about the pictures
- Point out words
- Use expression to bring the story to life
- Relate the story to their experiences
- Ask questions

Questions to Ask Toddlers

- "What do you think this story is about?"
- "What was the character's name?"
- "What word might come next?"
- "Does this remind you of…?"
- "When do we do this?"

Questions to Ask Young Children

- "What do you think this story will be about? Why?"
- "Where's the title?"
- "What's happened in the story so far?"
- "What might happen next?"
- "What does this mean?"

- "Why did the character do that?"
- "What would you do if you were the character?"

Questions to Ask Older Children

- "Why did you choose this book?"
- "What type of story is this?"
- "Who's your favorite character? Why?"
- "How do you know the character is feeling sad?"
- "Can you find a sentence that tells you about the setting?"
- "What was your favorite part of the book? Why?"
- "Does this book remind you of another story?"
- "Do you think the character made the right choice?"

You'll find that reading to your child is a naturally interactive experience, but these questions will give you an in-road to developing their comprehension skills. Discuss comparisons with their life and stories from your own life for an even richer experience and more engagement from your child.

★ Game Time!

What Really Happened? is a great game for developing your child's imagination and creativity. Choose a story they know well and enjoy, and ask them to make up a different ending.

For example, in *Goldilocks and the Three Bears*, Goldilocks sees the bear's house, but she decides to look in the shed. What happens next? Encourage your child to come up with solutions for problems and think about how the characters would behave.

7

CHATTERBOX: CONVERSATION IS MORE IMPORTANT THAN YOU MIGHT THINK

We started this journey off by talking about language development as the foundation for reading. If you want your child to get as much benefit as possible, talking is key. Research has shown that the number of words a child is exposed to from a young age is linked to their vocabulary development and reading comprehension later on.

TALKING TO LITTLE ONES

All conversation is good, and this begins from birth. Talking to your baby before they can respond is laying a strong foundation for literacy skills later. You'll probably find that this comes naturally to you, but it can seem a bit intimidating when you're looking at it through the lens of forwarding their language development. Here are a few pointers to help you on your way.

Talking to Your Baby

The easiest way to keep the conversation flowing with your baby is to describe their experiences and feelings. For example, when you know they're tired, you can say things like, "You're so fussy today. You're telling me you're tired. It's time for a nap." They won't understand your words, but they'll hear your tone, and they'll feel the love in your voice. Eventually, they'll come to understand what you're saying through repeated exposure.

Another trick is to copy the sounds your baby makes and encourage them to imitate you. You can put words to the sounds they make too: "I think you're telling me about the bird. Look at him flying so high! Hello, bird!"

Song is another useful tactic. You can make up songs about everyday experiences (and if that seems intimidating, just tweak a classic: "Happy bedtime to you!" (to the tune of *Happy Birthday*) or "Baa, baa, baby, is it time to sleep?" (to the tune of *Baa Baa Black Sheep*). The great thing about babies is that they have no idea if you're a good singer, so there's no reason to judge yourself. All they want is to hear your voice.

There are also a few games you can use to help lay the foundations for conversation later. Peek-a-boo is good for this: It's an example of turn-taking in its most simple form. Encouraging your baby to pass an object back and forth between you also sets up the turn-taking rules of conversation. And of course, you know the value of reading to them by now!

Talking to Your Toddler

It's almost difficult *not* to talk to a toddler. They demand conversation. Talk to them about what's happening when you're preparing a meal; encourage them to look for the biggest this or the smallest that. Ask them what color things are, and ask them questions that need a more developed answer than "Yes" or "No": "That's a pretty flower, isn't it? What else grows in the garden?"

"What if?" questions are great for toddlers too. "What would happen if we didn't tidy up?" Questions like this encourage them to think about the world around them and make sense of how different things relate.

Expose them to as many different experiences as you can, be they visits to the park, trips to the zoo, or playdates with friends. All of these events are great starting points for questions and answers.

Lastly, a sneaky way to show them the importance of books: When they inevitably ask a "But why?" question about something you don't know the answer to, say, "I don't know. Why don't we look it up?"

QUALITY MATTERS

While all talking is good, more recent research emphasizes the quality of the conversation you have with your child. A high-quality conversation is one that provides them with a good opportunity to build up their language skills. It's one in which both adult and child are engaged and enjoying the conversation, and it's one in which the adult takes their lead from the child, talking about what interests them. Both adult and child take turns, keeping the conversation flowing well.

BUILDING THEIR SKILLS THROUGH CONVERSATION

As your child gets older, there are a few specific strategies you can use in conversation to help them build up their vocabulary, comprehension, and critical thinking skills.

Introduce new vocabulary: If your child uses a simple word, try introducing them to a more sophisticated one. So, if they say, "His hat is big," you could say, "Yes! His hat's enormous!" Once you've done this, try to repeat the word in other situations to help your child become more familiar with it.

Expand their message: Take words and phrases your child uses, and turn them into complete sentences. For example, if they say, "Milk," you can say, "Yes, let's put some milk in your blue cup." What you're doing here is modeling the language they will use later.

Make recounts part of daily life: When you're visiting a familiar place, encourage your child to talk about what happened the last time you visited. Help them to clarify what they mean by asking questions. So, you might say, "Oh yes, we saw a fish in the tank, didn't we? What color was it?"

Make explanations part of daily life: As well as explaining things to your child, encourage them to think of explanations for things themselves. For example, if you're reading a story, you might ask, "Why do you think the dog is scared to leave his bone behind?"

Talk about what might happen next: Encourage your child to think about what will happen next in the day. If you're visiting the petting zoo, for example, you might ask, "What do you think will happen if we go to the fence? Do you think the donkey will come to us?" Wait for an answer, and then go over to the fence together to see if their prediction came true.

Help them to see other perspectives: Encourage your child to put themselves in someone else's shoes, whether that's another person or a character in a book. Ask them what they would do if they were in the same situation as the other person. This helps build both empathy and comprehension skills.

Involve them in problem-solving: When problems come up in day-to-day life, draw your child's attention to them and encourage them to come up with solutions. If you run out of milk, for example, ask them what you could do to solve the problem. If possible, give them a chance to try out their solution, even if there's a better one. So, with our milk example, if they suggest that you use orange juice instead, you might not want to waste a whole bowl of cereal, but you could say, "Oh, should we put orange juice on our cornflakes?" This will help them to think critically and understand how different elements of a situation interact.

I love talking as an illustration of the fact that nurturing literacy development really doesn't have to be a formal or complex affair. What builds your bond with your child also enhances their literacy development—it's win-win!

★ Game Time!

Going on a name safari around your house or your local area with your little one is a great opportunity for language building. Point out different objects, encouraging them to repeat the word. Let them lead the way, and if they point out something or ask what something is, give them the new word, and look for an opportunity to use it later.

SOMEONE LIKE YOU...

Unless someone like you cares a whole awful lot, nothing is going to get better. It's not.

— DR. SEUSS, *THE LORAX*

Learning starts with stories, songs, and play. It starts with exploration and adventure. It starts with writers like Dr. Seuss… and parents like you.

Yet despite this, we live in a world that teaches us fear. Are we good enough to help our children reach their potential? Are we doing everything we can?

I want to help parents give their children the very best start in life, but I also want to help squash that fear.

And you can help me to do that.

If you're browsing the internet for new books for your child, how do you choose? You look at reviews. You want to know about other people's experiences with each book. You want to know that other children have read and enjoyed it.

And that's also how we're going to help parents put their fear behind them and embrace the natural skills they already possess to help their child's reading journey.

If just one mom finds peace of mind, if just one child gets a more playful and natural introduction to reading, we've done something good.

How can you help? All you need to do is leave a short review. Just scan the QR code below!

Each honest review is a signpost for a parent who really wants to help their child, falling asleep each night safe in the knowledge that they've done the very best they could.

To go back to Dr. Seuss, *Unless someone like you cares a whole awful lot, nothing is going to get better. It's not.*

That act of caring will take you just a few minutes. I ask nothing from you but your honesty and your willingness to help other parents find the information they need.

From the bottom of my heart, thank you.

8

PLAYING WITH SOUND, RHYTHM, AND RHYME

There's a long tradition of singing nursery rhymes and songs to babies and young children for a reason, yet they're not as common now as they used to be. Rhythm and rhyme are important aspects of language and reading, and recognizing and playing with them will help your child's literacy development.

THE IMPORTANCE OF RHYME, RHYTHM, AND REPETITION

Rhyme, rhythm, and repetition are important for literacy skills because they allow children early access to language in a way that's easy for them to engage with. These devices help them to predict what will come next, highlighting particular sounds and therefore laying the foundations on which reading skills can later be built. Whether it's words, skills, or ideas that are repeated, repetition is a crucial part of early brain development, and it paves the way for learning. Rhyming, meanwhile, helps them to learn about sounds, words, and the way language is formed.

The Benefits of Rhyme for Babies

A baby's first experience of sound is a collection of noises that carry no meaning. In order to make sense of them and understand what they mean, they need to break that sound into meaningful units: words. This is where rhyme and rhythm come in. Babies are particularly sensitive to the rhythm in speech, and this is what allows them to segment the sound they hear into words. English is useful for this because over 90 percent of two-syllable words start with a stressed syllable, which alerts babies as young as nine months to the beginning of a new word. What the rhythm and rhyme we find in a nursery rhyme does is make those divisions more pronounced, supporting their language development.

This benefit isn't just found in nursery rhymes. Think of the way you talk to your baby. You probably use a lot of repetition and change your rhythm and pitch more dramatically than you would if you were speaking to an adult. You do this naturally because you get a better response from your baby, and at the same time, this is helping their vocabulary development, allowing them to distinguish between different words.

The Benefits of Rhyme for Toddlers and Preschoolers

Babies quickly become toddlers, but that response to rhyme and rhythm continues. Young children will often choose a rhyming book over a book that doesn't rhyme, taking pleasure in the strong rhythms they hear when you read to them. Both the rhythm of the text and the repetition make the language more predictable, and this means they're more likely to remember the words they hear. As they get older, they'll build up an awareness of rhyme, eventually being able to identify rhyming words and create their own. This paves the way for reading.

The rhythm found in nursery rhymes and rhyming stories helps children develop their listening skills, while the repetition helps them to build their vocabulary as they hear and memorize more words. Meanwhile, because rhyming stories and songs usually contain a narrative, they are being introduced to story structure.

EXPLORING RHYTHM AND RHYME WITH YOUNG CHILDREN

The way we naturally talk to young children, the use of nursery rhymes and songs in early years care, and the prevalence of rhythm and rhyme in children's books mean that children tend to be exposed to these linguistic devices regularly. Nonetheless, it's worth bearing in mind their importance, and seeking out activities that increase your child's exposure to them.

Activities for Younger Children

Nursery rhymes and songs are a great place to start. Encourage your child to join in, clapping, singing, or using simple percussion instruments like bells. As they become more proficient, you can encourage them to copy beats you make with a tambourine or shaker. Try to sing songs and use rhymes that include your child's name to capture their attention and encourage turn-taking.

You can easily build rhythm and rhyme into mundane activities too, making simple actions into songs ("This is the way we wash our hands, wash our hands, wash our hands…"), or singing and counting steps as you carry your little one down the stairs. This is very useful if you have a routine you want them to remember too: Repetition and rhyme will help them remember the important information.

And, of course, we have rhyming books. When they're familiar with a particular story, try leaving a gap for them to fill in the word that rhymes. From there, you can get creative with the words and come up with fun alternatives. For example, once your child is familiar with *Twinkle Twinkle Little Star*, you can come up with rhymes like, "Twinkle, twinkle, little pig, how I wonder why you dig."

Collect together objects with names that rhyme, talking to your child about their similarities and differences. A simple collection you could build at home, for example, might include a sock, a clock, and a lock. Can your child think of anything else they could add to the collection? "What about a rock? Where could we find a rock?"

You can also use fridge magnets to spell out word endings, and ask your child to put different letters in front of them to make rhyming words. You might start with the ending, "at"… What word will they make if they put a "b" at the front? How about a "c"?

Activities for Older Children

Rhythm, rhyme, and repetition are still useful as children get older. They continue to help them understand how language works, recognize regular patterns, and identify and memorize new words. Once they're writing, you can do things like write a single line of a poem and ask them to write the next line, aiming to keep the same rhythm and to rhyme the final word. You can also make a rhyming dictionary, adding new words as your child learns them. This is particularly useful once you get into more complex rhymes like "double" and "trouble."

Recommended Rhyming Books

There are so many brilliant rhyming books for children out there (with more being published every year) that it would be impossible to create a comprehensive list. Personally, I'm a big fan of Dr. Seuss. I can't think of a Dr. Seuss book my children haven't loved, and the rhymes and stories are so creative and engaging. Look in the children's section of any library or book shop, and you'll find an abundance of rhyming books. Be led by your child: Let them read the books *they* want to read. However, if you're looking for some good rhyming books to get your home collection started, here are a few popular ones to consider.

- *Duck in the Truck* (Jez Alborough)
- *Brown Bear, Brown Bear, What Do You See?* (Bill Martin, Jr.)
- *Sheep in a Jeep* (Nancy Shaw)
- *Is Your Mama a Llama?* (Deborah Guarino)
- *My Truck Is Stuck!* (Kevin Lewis)
- *Goodnight, Goodnight, Construction Site* (Sherri Duskey Rinker)
- *Sing to the Sun* (Ashley Bryan)
- *Mrs. McNosh Hangs up Her Wash* (Sarah Weeks)
- *Where Is the Green Sheep?* (Mem Fox)
- *The Random House Book of Poetry for Children* (edited by Jack Prelutsky)

The beauty of rhyming is that children absolutely love it, so as soon as you introduce the idea, they'll love finding ways to rhyme at every opportunity, and this only means good things for their literacy development. It's such an important tool for getting them to hear and understand the patterns in language, and it doesn't require any formal teaching at all. Just have fun with it, and your child will follow in your footsteps.

★ Game Time!

Finish the Sentence is a fun game to play with your child in the car, around the house, or to keep them occupied when you're grocery shopping. All you need to do is give them a sentence and ask them to make up the end with a word that rhymes: "The black cat is wearing a purple…?"

9

BUILDING SEQUENCING SKILLS

Sequencing is an important part of being able to read and understand text, so helping your child to develop this skill will be a huge asset to their reading journey. It allows them to recognize patterns they can use to understand the world around them. In relation to reading, it means they are able to see letters (and know their associated sounds) and put them together to form meaningful words. They are able to follow what happens in each part of a story, and understand that those parts must come in a particular order to make sense.

At a fundamental level, sequencing helps children learn routines and access important academic skills like investigation, problem solving, and reading comprehension.

HELPING CHILDREN TO DEVELOP SEQUENCING SKILLS

Again, sequencing is not something that requires formal teaching, and it can all be done through everyday activities and play. Perhaps you're already doing some of these activities with your child, but if you want to cover more bases, here are some good activities for helping them with their sequencing.

Do activities that naturally involve sequencing: Sequencing is naturally built into daily life; we just do it automatically as adults, so we don't always notice it. Involve your child in activities that involve sequencing, whether that's cooking, doing the laundry, or running a bath. Tell your child about what you're doing as you go, and ask them to tell you the order in which you took the steps.

Introduce sequencing words: When you're doing this, and at any other opportunity you have in ordinary life, introduce your child to words like "first," "next," "before," and "after": words that we use to sequence events. Once you introduce these words, use them as often as you can so your child becomes familiar with them. For example, if you're waiting to cross the road, you can talk about the cars in the line of traffic: "The first car is green, the second car is blue, and the last car is black." If you're baking with your child, you might say, "First we need to get the mixing bowl. Next, we need to weigh out the flour. Then we have to sift it." You're practicing sequencing and vocabulary building at the same time.

Talk about your day using sequencing words: A good way to practice using these new words is to talk about the things that have happened during your day: "First I took you to preschool. Then I went shopping. After that, I came home for lunch." You can also ask them about theirs: "What did you do first? What did you do after lunch?"

Use different modalities: You can practice sequencing with your child in a variety of different ways, which will help them improve their skills and interest in learning. You can use stories to show them how events happen in a particular order, asking them what happened first and what happened at the end. Singing and dancing, meanwhile, show your child the order of movements and actions, integrating sequencing into their activity. Pictures and objects can also be used to practice sequencing: building a tower made of alternating red and green blocks, for example, or stringing a repeating pattern of beads onto a thread.

Use sequencing cards: You can also buy sequencing cards that break down everyday activities into simple steps—things like brushing your teeth or washing your hands. There's no reason to buy them, of course—you can easily make your own by taking photos of your child completing the steps, and printing them out. Sequencing cards can be used for storytelling or as a visual reminder of what steps are needed in order to complete a task, and you can mix them up and ask your child to put them in the right order, modeling sequencing vocabulary as they do so: "First you put water on the toothbrush. Then you add toothpaste." You can also use them as a visual timetable to show your child what they can expect to happen during the day.

Talk about movies you've seen together: If you watch a film with your child, this presents a great opportunity to practice sequencing. Ask them if they can tell you the plot, and help them to put the events in order if they struggle.

As long as talking is a big part of your relationship with your child, sequencing is very easy to bring in naturally. Simply talking about your child's day at the dinner table is a great way to use sequencing naturally. I do this with all my kids—even the big ones! It's a great opportunity for bonding, but it also gives you the opportunity to model language use and help them sharpen their sequencing skills.

★ Game Time!

The Robot Game is one I used to like using at school for developing speech and language skills, but it works just as well at home. You are the robot, and you must follow your child's instructions very literally. For example, if your child tells you to put your hat on, the instruction is incomplete unless they tell you *where* to put it. You can make funny mistakes like putting your hat on the TV or on the teddy bear. Only when they tell you to put your hat on your head will you get it right. Sequencing language can also be incorporated in this game: What would your child like you to do next?

10

PRE-WRITING SKILLS (YES, THEY'RE IMPORTANT FOR READING TOO!)

It might seem strange to talk about writing before your child is even ready to read, but the two skills are intrinsically linked, and if you're aiming to give your child's literacy development a boost, it isn't just their pre-reading skills you want to focus on: It's also their pre-writing skills. This will directly benefit their reading skills, as they'll be able to access letters and early words in a different way, giving them a greater understanding of language and how it's used.

WHAT IS PRE-WRITING?

Just as pre-reading involves the foundational skills a child needs before they are able to read, pre-writing involves the skills they'll need in order to learn to write. Their gross motor control must be well developed, and they'll need good control over their core and posture. Just as with reading, they'll need to be able to cross the midline, and they'll need bilateral coordination, fine motor control, the ability to create simple patterns, and a good pencil grip. Let's look a little more closely at exactly what these skills involve.

Gross motor skills: These begin to form when a baby is born, and continue to develop well into childhood. Conveniently, the best way for this to happen is through play, which hopefully your child is already doing plenty of. When it comes time for them to write, they will need to have control over their body, and they will need to use their fine motor skills, which cannot be refined until they've developed that gross motor control. In fact, the other pre-writing skills they need won't be possible without a certain level of gross motor control in place.

Posture and core control: Writing requires us to have good control over our core, and the right posture to be able to sit in a certain position without becoming tired. Once they begin writing, children will need to sit up straight with their feet on the floor and their arms on the desk at right angles; until they are able to do this, writing will be difficult.

Crossing the midline: We discussed crossing the midline in relation to pre-reading skills, and it's just as significant when it comes to writing. In order to write on the left hand side of a piece of paper with their right hand (or vice versa if they're left-handed), they need to be able to cross the midline.

Fine motor skills: Writing requires a level of fine motor control that we don't have to think about as adults, but children need a lot of practice before they're ready to learn how to write. Over time, this will enable them to write without tiring, grip their pencil and form letters correctly, write neatly and in an appropriate size, and space out letters and words correctly.

Pencil grip: Before they can learn to write, children must have the ability to hold a pencil properly and apply the right level of pressure. They will need to control the pencil throughout the formation of letters and words without becoming tired.

Forming patterns: Children won't develop the control they need to form letters until they understand the shapes and patterns they find within those letters—and that comes long before letters are even introduced. Every time they do a puzzle, an activity involving shapes or pegs, or a drawing involving patterns, they're working on this skill. Once they are able, drawing patterns on a line (such as a zig-zag pattern) will mimic the movements needed to form letters when they learn to write.

PRE-WRITING ACTIVITIES FOR PRESCHOOLERS

Again, there's no need to formally teach pre-writing skills. There are plenty of fun and engaging activities you can build into ordinary life to allow your child to develop these skills in their own time.

Movement-Based Activities

Activities involving movement are key to helping your child develop their gross motor skills. As we've already seen in so many other areas, children naturally want to do this themselves, and it would actually be harder to stop them than it is to encourage them. Running, jumping, hopping, pulling, rolling, climbing, balancing, skipping, kicking... The list is endless, and all of these movements help them to develop control over their bodies. If you're looking for ideas beyond trips to the park and playing in the yard, consider singing songs and rhymes with actions, playing beanbag games, playing in the sandbox, hand-eye coordination games, building games, and arts and crafts activities. Bear in mind that they will also need to build up strength in their hands in order to write. Playing with playdough and scrunching up paper are great for this.

Activities to Develop Fine Motor Skills

Although gross motor skills are essential to developing fine motor skills, the two develop in tandem. Again, play is key here, and they will naturally work on these skills any time they're playing in the sandbox or drawing a picture. You can also try painting, cutting and tearing activities, puzzles, pegboards, and threading and beading activities.

Playing with Letters

We've already mentioned alphabet fridge magnets, but letters and numbers made from foam, plastic, or wood are more great tools to have at your disposal. These introduce your child to writing (and reading) in a fun and tactile way. Encourage your child to touch them and trace the letter formation with their finger (you can guide them) to familiarize themselves with how each letter is formed.

Pattern-Forming Activities

There's no point in introducing these activities until your child is able to hold a pencil properly without tiring, and this should not be rushed. Keep an eye on their drawing and coloring, and you'll know when they might be ready for this. Pencil grip is difficult to correct when children have grown accustomed to an incorrect grip, so it's worth buying some rubber pencil grips when they're starting out. These guide their fingers to the right place on the pencil, and can later be removed when you're confident your child can maintain a good grip.

You can use a large piece of paper for this, or you could make it a fun outdoor activity in the yard using brightly colored chalk. Encourage your child to scribble in zig-zag movements, moving the chalk or crayon up and down and left and right. Make large circular patterns, taking the chalk in both directions (this mimics the way we form letters like "b" and "d"). Explore wave patterns and straight line patterns. As your child's motor control develops and they have a good grasp of these patterns, you can move onto regular-sized paper, encouraging them to form smaller patterns like in the example below.

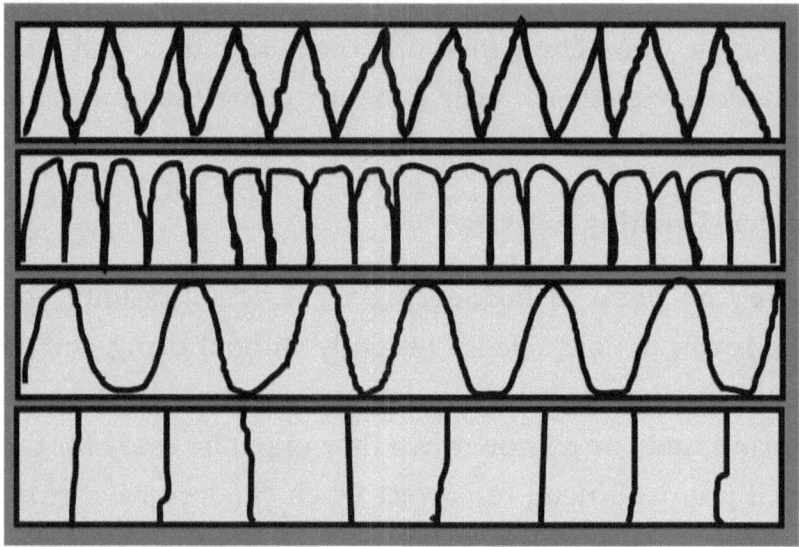

Pre-writing Shapes

The ability to form pre-writing shapes can be done in tandem with making patterns, but again, should not be rushed, and children will need a good pencil grip before they are ready. Pre-writing shapes are the shapes and lines involved in writing—the same ones you're using in pattern making. They include curved and straight lines, and directional movements (vertical, horizontal, and diagonal lines). Shapes like + and x teach children to intersect lines, while triangles and squares show them how to draw corners. Both of these skills will be important for writing later.

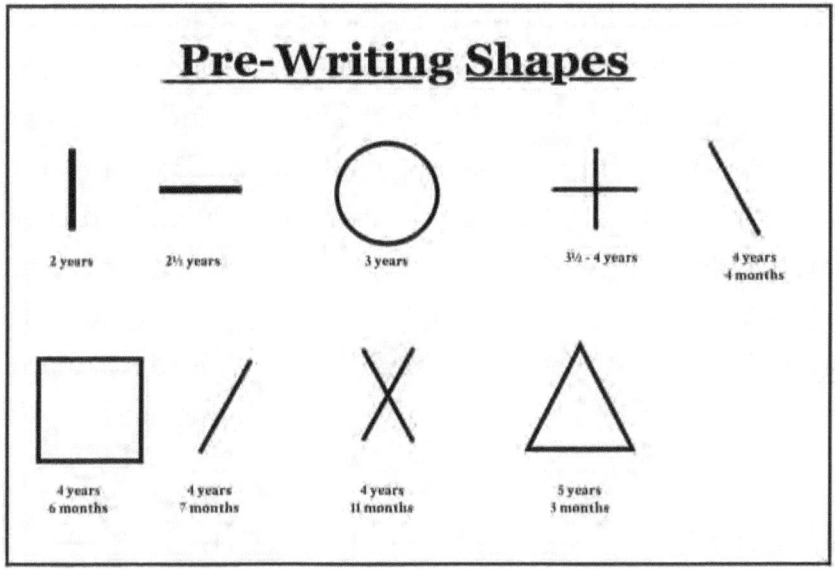

In the diagram above, you can see the pre-writing shapes and the approximate age at which children learn to draw them. Again, I can't stress enough that this is only a guideline. Children develop at different rates, and in this case, only 50 percent of children will draw the shapes at the age associated with them. That means a further 50 percent of children are going to develop more slowly than this.

TRANSITIONING TO WRITING

Only when a child has mastered pattern making and pre-writing shapes are they ready to start forming letters. These are usually introduced on a large piece of paper or on a board, and children start practicing them on a large scale. They then move on to forming those letters on paper, learning how to start in the correct place and follow the right direction for each letter. At this stage they also learn about leaving a space between each letter. Once they have mastered this, they begin combining letters to form words and separating those words with spaces. From there come sentences and basic punctuation, and later, paragraphs. None of this is anything you need to worry about before your child starts school. Your child is going to learn to write. That's what school is there for. Your job is to make sure they have foundations in place to fly when they get there.

MAKING WRITING A NATURAL PART OF THE DAY

Your child may not be ready to write yet, but that doesn't mean that they can't benefit from having writing be a part of everyday life. When they're drawing, talk about what they've drawn. Ask questions and show your enthusiasm. If they have attempted to draw letters but they've missed the mark, don't mention it. Simply encourage their attempts, and eventually, correctly formed letters will emerge. Responding to your child's early mark making tells them that writing conveys meaning, and this will entice them to want to learn how to do it. Let them see you writing too: shopping lists, notes to family members, information on the calendar… This is all modeling to them how writing is used, and it tells them that it has value.

Literacy is the whole picture of reading, writing, and comprehending language. Helping your child with their pre-writing skills will have a knock-on effect on their reading. Once they begin to write letters, you can tie this into practicing letter sounds and names. My youngest, Ava, is now at the stage where she sounds out the letters as she writes them. It's totally adorable to watch, and it's a really clear illustration of how closely reading and writing are linked.

★ Game Time!

Okay, so it's less a game and more an activity… but your child will have loads of fun doing it. All you'll need is a bag of beads in a variety of shapes and colors, and some pipe cleaners. Your child can practice their sequencing skills and develop their fine motor skills at the same time by threading beads onto the pipe cleaner in a pattern. They will need to use a pincer grip in order to do this, and this will help them develop the finger strength and dexterity they'll need to control a pencil.

A WORLD OF WORDS: RECOGNIZING PRINT IN THE ENVIRONMENT (AND ADDING YOUR OWN!)

Print is all around us. That, indeed, is one of the reasons that literacy is so important: It's a valuable tool for making sense of the world. But that print all around us is a tool in itself, and helping children to recognize and understand it is an important part of nurturing confident and fluent readers.

ENVIRONMENTAL PRINT

The signs, symbols, logos, and words we see around us every day are examples of environmental print—everything from the stop sign, to the McDonald's logo, to the street sign at the end of the road. Your child is exposed to these things every day, and drawing their attention to them helps them to build print awareness.

Building Print Awareness

Making your child aware of environmental print is as simple as talking to them about it when you see it. If you're driving with them in the car, draw their attention to the road signs and talk about what they mean. Talk about the labels on your grocery items. This is a valuable opportunity to teach life lessons too: "Why does the cleaning chemical have a warning sign on it?" "How can we find out how much sugar is in this cookie?"

You can also use opening the mail as a teachable moment: "Who are these letters from?" "How did I know this letter was for me?" And of course, you can also use books: "How do we know who the author is?" "Which part tells us what the book is called?"

When you're playing with your child, draw their attention to the print around them. If they want to play shop, consider letting them stock their shelves with unopened packets of food, and take the opportunity to draw their attention to the words and logos. Help them to make signs for different parts of their store, and use this as a starting point for a conversation about why signs are important.

Taking It a Step Further

You can take this a step further by encouraging your child to make a collection of environmental print. Whether it's in a scrapbook or on a large piece of paper, they can cut out familiar symbols and logos from newspapers and magazines, and stick them in their collection. You could also take photos of different signs in your neighborhood, or you could cut out the print from old cereal boxes and labels. You could even sort the signs out, grouping together ones that begin with the same letter of the alphabet, or identifying the signs with an /a/ sound in them.

Making Your Home Rich in Words

A good way to extend the benefits of environmental print is to add it to your own home. It isn't, strictly speaking, environmental print, but it has the same effect: It's exposure to words and letters.

Add alphabet posters to your child's bedroom walls (or create an alphabet poster together). Label the pictures they draw. For example, if they draw a dog, you can write "This is a dog," and display it on the wall. Let them watch you make your shopping list, and look at magazines and newspapers with them. If they seem interested in a picture, read out the caption underneath it.

Really, any way you can get the written word into your home is valuable. Let them see that words are friendly and useful, and they'll naturally build an interest in learning how to make sense of them.

Print is everywhere. Help your child to tune into it, and encourage them to ask questions and recognize patterns. The chances are, they already recognize the McDonald's logo. Use this as a jumping off point: "What letter is it?" "Why does it mean McDonald's?" The funny thing is, the more you build up your child's awareness, the more aware of environmental print you become yourself. It really does bring home how important reading and writing are. Our world revolves around them.

★ Game Time!

Memory Match Cereal Boxes: For this, you'll need two each of several kinds of mini-cereal boxes. Cut off the front of each box, mix up the cards, and arrange them face down on a table. You've just created an environmental-print based memory matching game, and this will help your child with their literacy skills without them even noticing.

12

IGNITING AN EVERLASTING LOVE OF BOOKS

Your main goal is to foster a love of reading in your child… and that means making sure they have books to love. That doesn't mean you have to go out there and spend a fortune though. There are plenty of ways you can increase your child's exposure to books without spending a dollar. The library is my personal favorite, mostly because all my kids love it so much. I love taking them to choose a new book, and I love watching them explore the shelves, looking for something that speaks to them. Beyond that, consider thrift stores, garage sales, and book swaps. No one said a book has to be new for it to be great.

THE SEARCH FOR A GOOD BOOK

Since you'll be sharing reading time with your child, I'd aim for books that both of you will love. Of course, this doesn't mean you shouldn't follow your child's lead and let them choose what interests them, but you can always do a bit of gentle steering too. Ask your friends and other parents what their favorite books are, and if you're visiting the library, ask the librarian about popular titles. Keep an eye on book reviews, and look out for award-winning titles—these usually have a sticker on the front, so you'll spot them easily. Bear in mind that your child's listening level is different from their reading level, so even if they're beginning to read simple books, you'll probably want to choose a more advanced book for story time. This will encourage a love of reading and help you motivate them to keep on learning.

One thing I would say about any book you choose: Don't be afraid to give up on it if your child isn't enjoying it. Forcing them to listen to a story they're not interested in won't help them to love reading; it will have entirely the opposite effect. Use it as an opportunity for conversation: "I don't really like this one either. Why do you think that is? What sort of story would you prefer to read?" This is a good way of developing their comprehension skills too.

Reading should be exciting. Children want to hear stories that make them feel things, that reflect their experiences, that take them to imaginary worlds. They want to hear playful language and catchy rhythms. As soon as they're not enjoying a book, it's time to give up. I can think of several books I've given up on as an adult. Some books just don't work for everyone, and we want to give children the freedom to follow their own interests. That's what will foster a lifelong love of reading.

CHOOSING BOOKS FOR DIFFERENT AGE GROUPS

I preface this by reminding you that I use the term "age groups" loosely here. Think of them more as developmental stages. Perhaps your five year old is still at the preschool stage: That's totally fine. Look for books that address their developmental stage rather than their age group. I also want to remind you that every child's taste is different, so view these pointers as guidelines rather than rules. I've included a few suggestions for each age group, but there are so many more out there. These are really just tiny drops in a vast ocean.

Books for Babies and Toddlers

Babies are drawn to brightly colored books containing colorful pictures of simple objects. Look for books with good rhythm and simple language, but also include books without words at all: books that stimulate them on a mental and a visual level. Toddlers love these books too because they can create their own stories, and they provide a great opportunity for discussion. Look for indestructible books, or at least those that are a bit more hardwearing: Think board books, plastic books, and cloth books.

A Few Suggestions

- *Chicka Chicka Boom Boom* (Bill Martin, Jr.)
- *The Very Hungry Caterpillar* (Eric Carle)
- *Goodnight Moon* (Margaret Wise Brown)
- *Hip-Hop Lollipop* (Susan Montanari and Brian Pinkney)
- *Bear Moves* (Ben Bailey Smith and Sav Akyüz)

Books for Preschool and Kindergarten

Children at this stage enjoy listening to slightly more difficult text with a good rhythm and lots of repetition. Nursery rhymes are a good choice, as are books that involve familiar experiences and objects. Interactive books with pop-up components or moving parts are good fun too, and they can help capture a child's attention and encourage them to be involved in the story.

A Few Suggestions

- *Where the Wild Things Are* (Maurice Sendak)
- *Corduroy* (Don Freeman)
- *Swimmy* (Leo Lionni)
- *Press Here* (Hervé Tullet)
- *Ada Twist, Scientist* (Andrea Beaty and David Roberts)

Books for 5–8 Year Olds

Most children begin to learn to read in the first grade, but some children will have been ready to start earlier, and some may still not be ready. Either way, I'd recommend that you continue to read *to* your child for pleasure. We've already covered the vast benefits of this, and if you're able to read them stories more complex than the ones they can read for themselves, they're more likely to develop a love of books. Choose picture books with good stories and character development, and remember that their listening comprehension will be more sophisticated than their reading comprehension.

If your child is reading independently, supplement your shared story books with simple stories with familiar words. Look for stickers like "Easy Reader," which signpost that the material will be accessible to early readers. For more accomplished readers (probably around the third grade), you might want to choose slightly more complex stories which include a few challenging words alongside lots of familiar language. Remember to include some non-fiction texts too.

A Few Suggestions

- *Juana & Lucas* (Juana Medina)
- *Mercy Watson* (Kate Dicamillo)
- *Charlie and Mouse* (Laurel Snyder)
- *Peter and Ernesto* (Graham Annable)
- *Mighty Robot* (Dav Pilkey)

Books for Children Aged 9+

Encourage children at this stage to choose their own books, but monitor their choices to make sure they're challenging themselves. The personality and preferences are important factors in book selection, and reading material should be accessible, yet contain a few challenging ideas and words.

Quite a lot of publishers include an age group on the covers of their books. Use these to help you out, but don't be afraid to choose a book that's aimed higher or lower. You know your child, and the book you share together during story time doesn't need to be a book they could read independently.

I've left the suggestions out here, partly because your child's personality is so important at this stage, and partly because so many ages and stages could be included.

If children are to have a good relationship with reading, they need to enjoy the process, and that starts with the material they have to read. When they're little, you may find that they have particular favorites they want to read over and over again. That's okay, and shouldn't be discouraged. Just try to add a few new books into the mix as well.

★ Game Time!

Story Clouds: All you need is a nice cloudy day and a bit of free time. Take your child outside and lie down on the grass, looking for pictures in the clouds. When you've found a few, encourage your little one to tell a story, linking all the pictures together. I love doing this just as much as my kids do… and he'd probably hate me for telling you, but my ten year old still loves it too!

LET'S TELL A STORY: WRITING STORIES TOGETHER

Storytelling can be done before a child is able to read or write, and it's a great way to build their confidence and spark their interest. I still remember a story my son made up when he was very little. I was utterly amazed by the vocabulary I had no idea he knew. There was a cat who yawned wearily, and someone stepped over a threshold. All those fairytales obviously paid off!

MAKING UP STORIES FOR YOUR CHILD

A great place to start is to tell your own stories. Children love to copy what they see their parents do, so if you make up stories, they'll be encouraged to do the same. I agree that this can be a bit intimidating if it's new to you, but the reason many parents don't try is simply that they don't feel like they're creative enough. My best advice is to not overthink it. Keep it simple. Start with the setting, then think of a character, and then come up with a goal that the character wants to achieve. You might have a magical bear in an icy cave who wants to find a new friend. Children love it when they're included in a story, so consider naming your main character after them, or add them into the story. Perhaps your child hears the bear crying and comes to ask what's wrong. Keep the story short, and if you get stuck, borrow ideas from children's films and books. You can even ask your child to join in: "What do you say to the bear?"

Once your child shows an interest in telling their own stories, ask them questions and give them prompts to help them through the narrative. You can say things like, "What happened next?" or "And then what did he do?" Give your child your full attention, and show your enthusiasm. If they see that you're interested, they'll be encouraged to keep going. Ask them to explain if the story gets confusing. This will help them understand that storytelling is a form of communication, and that there is a relationship between the person telling the story and the person hearing it.

Story Prompts to Get You Started

If you're struggling for ideas for stories and you're looking for something more complex, often a prompt is all you need to get you off the ground. Here are a few ideas to get you going.

Quest: One sunny afternoon, [Character] was walking in the woods when they discovered an old map. An [exciting object] was marked on the map. There was just one problem: To find the treasure, they'd have to get past the [villain/obstacle].

Example: One sunny afternoon, James was walking in the woods when he discovered an old map. A magical gemstone was marked on the map. There was just one problem: To find the treasure, James would have to get past the evil troll.

Chaos: [Character] was at the fair with their friends, when suddenly a [surprising thing] fell out of the sky.

Example: Lorrie was at the fair with her friends, when suddenly a sad robot with purple hair fell out of the sky.

Adapting a classic: Once upon a time, [Character] skipped through the woods with a basket of cakes for her grandmother.

I think you can manage without an example for that one!

WRITING STORIES TOGETHER

Once your child is confident in making up stories of their own, you can move on to writing a story together. Older children may want to write, but children at an earlier developmental stage may need to dictate to you. Ask your child to tell you a story, whether that's a fictional creation from their own imagination, or a recount of an outing you've had together. Write the story down as they tell it, ideally on a large piece of paper in a bright color. You may need to make the odd change to their sentences in order for it to make grammatical sense, but keep the content the same, and then read the story back to them so they can hear how it sounds. Your child can then illustrate the story, and you can display it on a wall to encourage a sense of pride and help them see that writing has a purpose.

Storytelling takes the pressure off reading and writing while simultaneously strengthening literacy and language skills. It's also a lot of fun, and a great opportunity for bonding. If you feel self-conscious at first, try to work through it. Your child isn't judging you, and they'll be far more disappointed if you give up. Instead, enlist their help and make it fun.

★ Game Time!

Story Building: Come up with a sentence to introduce a story (e.g., "Once upon a time, there was a furry blue monster.") Ask your child to add a sentence. Perhaps they say, "The monster was looking for his ball." Now it's your turn to add a sentence. Use your sentence to challenge your child to think outside the box. You might say, "All of a sudden, a big crash came out of nowhere and startled the monster." Ask your child to add the next line. This can go on for as long as you want it to, and more often than not, ends up in a ridiculous story and a lot of laughter. It's brilliant for developing their imagination and helping them think about story structure.

14

LEARNING THE LETTER SOUNDS

There's a difference between teaching children the names of the letters and teaching them the letter sounds. The letter names are important to know, but the sounds are actually more important for reading. This is the basis for a phoneme-based reading approach, and it's what they'll build on later. However, this isn't to say that teaching them the letter names isn't important. In order to read, they need to understand what is known as "the alphabetic principle"—that is, they need to understand that letters represent the sounds we hear in spoken language. It is understanding that sounds and letters have a relationship that will allow them to decode new words and read, eventually, with fluency.

UNDERSTANDING THE ALPHABETIC PRINCIPLE

If they are to have a good understanding of the alphabetic principle, children need to learn the names of the letters first. If their alphabetic knowledge is underdeveloped, they'll struggle to learn the letter sounds. Alphabetic knowledge is acquired in sequence, starting with letter names, progressing to the shapes of the letters, and ending with the letter sounds.

Learning Letter Names

There are a few good strategies you can employ for teaching your child the letter names. Alphabet songs are a great one. There's the classic alphabet song that comes up in most preschools and childcare facilities, but there are also plenty of others you can easily find online.

A good approach to teaching children any skill is to reach them on a number of different channels, though, so it's a good idea to supplement your singing with other resources. Letter-matching games work well. You'll need a mat or poster with the letters of the alphabet on it, and letter shapes or magnets that correspond in size. Ask your little one to match the shape in their hand with its counterpart on the poster.

A bit of stealth-teaching never goes amiss either. Alphabet noodles, alphabet soup, alphabet cookies… Any alphabet-shaped food you can find is a good teaching tool. You can also use alphabet cookie cutters if you're baking with your little one. Ask them if they can find the letter their name begins with, or ask them which letter they're about to eat. Liam used to love alphabet food when he was little. He would always eat all the Ls first, and he loved asking us how to make words out of his noodles.

Lastly, remember that environmental print is all around you. The world is full of opportunities for asking your child if they can spot a letter R or find a red B. It's a great way to keep them occupied on a car ride too!

A Word on Vowels and Consonants

It will also help children to know which letters are vowels and which are consonants. This doesn't need to involve formal instruction—you can just include it as part of your conversation about letters. At the risk of sounding like a broken record, magnetic fridge letters are great for this. You can keep the vowels separately in their own space on the fridge so that children become familiar with them. If you can have them in a separate color from the other letters, all the better.

The song *Old MacDonald Had a Farm* is a great vowel-teaching tool too. The verse traditionally goes, "Old MacDonald had a farm, e-i-e-i-o." Try changing this to include the names of the vowels instead: "Old MacDonald had a farm, a-e-i-o-u." It works a bit like a mnemonic, in that it will give your child a peg for the memory of the vowel names.

MOVING ON TO LETTER SOUNDS

Once children are familiar with the letters and their names, they're ready to learn the letter sounds. This will need to be done for each letter in isolation, and it will require you to tell them explicitly what sound each letter makes. Don't panic: We'll get to some strategies for doing this a little further down the chapter. From here, give them the opportunity to practice, asking them what sound a letter makes when you encounter it, and what letter makes a /b/ sound, for example.

It may be tempting to teach the letter sounds in alphabetical order, but I'd advise against it. There are a couple of reasons for this. Firstly, your child is more likely to get the letter's name than its sound if you teach it in alphabetical order. Secondly, you want to start with letters that are used more frequently in the text they'll come across.

Different teaching programs use different orders for teaching letter-sound correspondence. If you already know what school your child will be attending, you may want to use the order they use in their phonics teaching, but this isn't necessary. All programs work on the principle of teaching more frequently used sounds first.

My preference is to start with the SATPIN method, which is simply to begin with the letters S, A, T, P, I, and N, the six letters that begin most phonics programs. The reason for this is that these sounds combine to make the most words, so they give children the quickest access to practicing reading and using their knowledge. From there, I build in groups of sounds that support the first group, allowing them to access more CVC (consonant-vowel-consonant) words, and leaving the least commonly used letters for last. For quick reference, this is the order in which I like to teach the letter sounds. This is the order I've used in school, and it's what I've done with my own children.

S, A, T, P, I, N

C, O, D, G, M, K

E, R, U, B, H, F, L

J, W, V, X, Y, Z, Q

Although the letter sounds need to be taught explicitly and in isolation, this doesn't mean you should introduce only one new one at a time. You don't want to overload them, but introducing a few new letters each at a time is a good move. Wait until your child is comfortable with all the sounds in a group before you introduce the next collection. I'd recommend focusing on lower case letters to begin with, as these are what they'll see more frequently.

Trip Hazards to Watch Out For

I don't want to spend too long talking about problems because you can't do a lot of harm here. However, there are a couple of things worth watching out for when you begin teaching your child the letter sounds.

The first of those is the schwa. The schwa is a linguistic concept that we could discuss in great detail, but it's only relevant to you in that it's easy to accidentally add to the ends of sounds if you're not careful. It most commonly sounds like a short /u/ sound, and it becomes problematic if you teach the letter sounds with it at the end. So, for example, what you want your child to hear is a clean /b/ sound, not /bu/. The reason this is important is that it can interfere with reading when children come to blend sounds to make words. If they misunderstand the letter "b" to make a /bu/ sound, the word "bat" will be segmented into the sounds /bu/ /a/ /t/, and they won't be able to blend the sounds to find a word with meaning. They will need the sounds /b/ /a/ /t/ in order to do this.

The second thing to watch out for is the different sounds that vowels make. In some words, the vowels have a short sound—as in the words "bat," "pet," "dip," "cot," and "cup." Start by teaching them these sounds. These are the ones they'll encounter first in their reading, the kind seen in CVC words. There are other words in which vowels make a long sound, or to put it simply, they "say their name." Think of the "a" in "came" or "hate." There are other spelling rules at play in these cases, and your child doesn't need to know these when they're starting out. Some teachers use the distar alphabet, which represents long-sound vowels with a line over the top of the letter. This is helpful for teaching vowels, but you don't really need to use it at home. Just start with the short vowel sounds, and we can build from there.

While we're discussing long vowel sounds, I just want to mention two other concepts you may come across. These are digraphs and trigraphs. Digraphs are pairs of letters used to represent a single sound—for example "ch" and "sh." Trigraphs are trios of letters that do the same thing—for example "igh" or "air." These sounds will need to be taught too, as children need to understand that the letters in them follow different rules. In the word "ship," for example, they will need to blend the sounds /sh/ /i/ and /p/—not /s/ /h/ /i/ and /p/. We'll look at this in more detail in Chapter Seventeen.

EASY AND FUN WAYS TO TEACH THE LETTER SOUNDS

Before we go further, I'd just like to remind you that you don't need to give your child formal instruction in order to teach them the letter sounds. As a parent of a preschooler, what you want to do is build it into daily life in a fun way. To them, it will feel more like play and exploration than anything else, and I think this is important. You don't want them to feel any pressure, and you don't want to do anything to harm the love of reading that you've been nurturing until this point. The good news is that teaching your child the sounds that the letters make is really straightforward, and there are plenty of tools you can use to help you.

All of the methods I'm about to list are methods I've worked with in school or used with my own children, and they're all useful approaches. Again, aim for a multifaceted approach, including teaching opportunities at any moment they arise and making the experience as varied and fun for your child as possible.

Tactile learning: I love using a tactile approach to teaching the letter sounds because it engages a child's sense of touch, which can help them build a stronger connection with the sound they're learning. What's more, the options are almost endless, and they're all lots of fun. Let's say you want to teach them the letter "s." Write this out in large, bold lettering, and then equip them with kinetic sand, play dough, shaving foam, or any other resource they can manipulate. Say the letter sound out loud while your child makes a copy (or builds it on top of your letter) using the material you've given them, and encourage them to say the sound too. If you're using shaving foam or sand, your child can trace the letter in it while they say the sound.

Linking to familiar symbols: This is a useful way to build letter-sound correspondence into everyday life. Use things that your child is already familiar with to increase their engagement and make them feel comfortable. Let's say you want to teach the sound of the letter "t." Look for objects or pictures of objects that begin with a /t/ sound that your child already loves. Perhaps you have toy tigers and trucks and pictures of tomatoes, toast, and toys. Anything that starts with a /t/ sound is fair game. You can collect pictures of /t/ words with your child and build up a booklet together. It's a fun craft activity, and it's a way to increase your child's understanding of how the letter sounds work.

Repetition: Repetition is key to learning new concepts, and letter sounds are no different. Introduce the sounds in the order we discussed earlier, and don't introduce a new group until your child is familiar with the first. Through continually hearing the same letter sounds repeated, your child is more likely to grasp a firm understanding. One thing I've done with my own kids is to have a "letter jar." Every week, we would have a different letter, clearly visible in a glass jar in the hallway. They loved coming downstairs on a Monday to see what the new letter was. Ask your child to point out words starting with that letter throughout the week, and give them a special ticket to put in the jar every time they find one (I just used raffle tickets). Challenge them to see if they can get three tickets a day. This is a great way to build repetition easily into the day, and a fun way to teach the letter sounds without any formal lessons.

Digital letters: We could easily get distracted by the argument that children spend too much time with technology these days, but the keys of a keyboard or touch screen are a great teaching tool, and I think there's a real value in introducing your child to letters as they'll see them when they come to write on computers later on. Try calling out the letter sounds you're working on and asking your child to find the matching letter on the keyboard. Bear in mind that the letters on the majority of external keyboards are in upper case, so your child will need to be familiar with both upper and lower case letters before they can do this with a computer. Your other devices should be fine though.

Bingo: Some games never get old, and Bingo, it seems, is one of them. To use it to practice letter-sound correspondence with your child, print out a Bingo sheet with pictures of familiar objects. Call out a letter sound your child has been working on, and ask them to cross off the picture of an object beginning with that sound. Once all the pictures have been checked off, they've won. This is good if you have big kids too—my older two love playing sound Bingo with their little sister.

Letter cards: I want to include these because they're a useful resource, but I think it's important not to rely on them. Your child is going to see plenty of letter cards when they start school, and you want to avoid making your home feel like a formal learning environment. However, they're particularly useful when you first introduce your child to a new letter sound, and they're a valuable tool to have in your arsenal. Once your child is secure in a few sounds, try holding up the cards and asking them to say the correct one for each letter.

You could also hide a selection of cards in a bag, and ask your child to pull out a card and tell you what sound the letter makes.

Learning the letter names is important to your child understanding the alphabetic principle, but it's vital that they learn the sounds those letters make too. Teaching them this gives them an important key for decoding words later on.

★ Game Time!

Go Fish: This classic game is really useful for practicing letter sounds. You could either play it with letter cards, or you could use cards that show familiar objects. Give your child five cards, and put the rest on the table. Call out a letter sound, and ask your child if they have a match (whether that's the corresponding letter or a picture of an object that begins with the sound). If they don't have a matching card, they must take a new card from the pile.

15

HEARING THE SOUNDS IN WORDS

To become a confident and fluent reader, your child will need to not only match a letter with its sound, but also to be able to hear that sound in a word. This is called "phonological awareness"—an awareness of the sounds in language. Luckily, this is really easy to practice at home, and feeds back into consolidating their understanding of letter sounds. It also crosses over with a lot of the other areas we've looked at, so it can easily be integrated into most activities.

UNDERSTANDING PHONOLOGICAL AWARENESS

Good phonological awareness requires your child to be able to hear and understand the sounds within words. This means they'll need to be able to recognize and create rhymes, identify the sounds at the beginnings and ends of words, break words into their separate syllables, blend sounds and syllables to make words, and manipulate the sounds found in words.

These skills can't develop until your child has certain foundations in place, which reaffirms the importance of the pre-reading phase. There's no sense in rushing children to read before they're ready: They simply won't have the necessary skills in place for it to be successful. They need to have developed their attention and concentration skills to a level that they can focus on an activity without distraction, and their auditory processing skills need to be developed to the extent that they can separate relevant sounds from background sounds and distinguish between similar ones. They also need to be able to understand concepts like "beginning," "middle," and "end," and their working memory needs to be strong enough to retain and manipulate the language they hear.

HELPING YOUR CHILD TO HEAR THE SOUNDS IN WORDS

If only it were as simple as simply being able to hear. But unfortunately, children need to learn and practice hearing the sounds in language. However, this is very easy to instigate with fun activities and games, and doesn't require formal teaching. Best of all, if you've already been reading to your child, singing to them, and making talking an important part of everyday life, you've been working on this skill already. Every time you're reading a nursery rhyme and drawing their attention to the sounds of letters and words, they're building up their phonological awareness.

Here are a few other ideas to give them a little boost.

Counting words: Verbally give your child a sentence and ask them to count how many words you said. This will help them to identify the separate words and relate the sounds to individual units of meaning.

Rhyming games: Try playing a version of *I Spy* in which your child has to spy an object that rhymes with a particular word (e.g., "I spy with my little eye something that rhymes with *hat*." You can also change this up so that they have to find objects that begin or end with a particular sound.

Rhythm games: Give your child a percussion instrument and ask them to make a beat when they hear or say each word in a sentence. As they grow more comfortable, they can do this for syllables or sounds. This can also be done by clapping.

Missing syllables and sounds: Say a word, and leave off the last syllable (e.g., "libra_") and ask them to finish the word: "library." Clap out the syllable rhythm in different words to help them hear the syllables. You can also remove individual sounds from words and ask them what word would be left. For example, "If you take the /p/ sound away from 'pat,' what word is left?"

CLUES THAT YOUR CHILD IS STRUGGLING

I think it's helpful to be aware of the signs that a child is having difficulties with phonological awareness, but I don't want you to worry too much about this. There are interventions that can help once your child starts school, and struggling now doesn't necessarily mean there will be an ongoing problem. It could also simply mean that they're developing a little more slowly than their peers, and this is totally fine.

At the preschool stage, if your child struggles to recognize or come up with rhyming words, they can't hear the first sound in a word, or they can't identify the separate syllables making up a word, they may be struggling with their phonological awareness.

At this stage, all you need to do is keep nurturing those pre-reading skills. Keep on reading. Keep on singing. Keep on talking. Do everything we've talked about up until this point, and don't worry. Once your child starts school, you'll know to be aware of it and address it with their teacher if they don't catch up.

There are two things I love about this part of the process. 1.) You're working on it within everything you're already doing to support your child's literacy. 2.) It can be done anywhere at any time. Everything's an opportunity. I remember I was once stuck in traffic for well over an hour with Amelia, and we spent the whole time playing sound games. We hardly noticed how much time we'd spent going nowhere!

★ Game Time!

Sound Race: You'll need a bit of space for this one, but I like it as a way to make language games more active. Pin two letter cards to different trees in your yard. Give your child a simple word (e.g., "dog") and ask them to run to the sound they hear at the start of the word. Ask them to say the sound when they reach the tree. You can adapt this game according to your space, and you can also change the rules to practice hearing the last or middle sound in a word.

16

MANIPULATING SOUNDS

The ability to manipulate phonemes (units of sound) is another key skill needed in reading, and this builds on your child's ability to hear sounds in words. When we talk about phoneme manipulation, we're simply talking about the ability to add and delete sounds in words, and this is easily built into the activities you've already been doing with your child.

STRATEGIES FOR PRACTICING PHONEME MANIPULATION

Sound deletion: Ask your child to say words without some of their sounds. It's a good idea to start with the initial sound in a word, and only when they're secure in this, move on to deleting middle or final sounds. Ask your child to try saying "pat" without the /p/ sound, and move on from here.

Sound substitution: Once your child is confident about deleting sounds, ask them to change the sounds to make new words. For example, "Can you change 'pat' into 'sat'?" or "What happens if we swap the /p/ sound in 'pat' with a /s/ sound?" Kids have a delightful sense of humor, so there's no reason to use real words every time.

Silly sounds: You can build on this and continue to use humor to engage your child in sound play. Choose a category (e.g., animals), and choose something within that category (e.g., horse). Ask your child to change the first sound to make silly new words—so "horse" might become "borse," "torse," "porse," etc.

Changing sounds: An extension of silly sounds is to challenge your child to change the initial sound to produce only real words. So, "red" might become "bed," "fed," or "shed," but it can't become "ked."

All of these activities can be done verbally without props, but you could also use letters written on sticky notes, magnetic letters, or whiteboard markers to add visual and physical stimulation. This will also help consolidate their understanding of the relationship between sounds and letters.

Once children get the hang of this, they tend to really enjoy playing silly word games, so it can be quite rewarding when they get to this stage. My youngest, Ava, thinks it's hilarious to change the first sound in any word anyone says at the dinner table. She drives her siblings crazy, but it's great practice. Children do a lot of these things naturally when you give them the right tools.

★ Game Time!

Guess My Word: Give your child the sounds in a simple word and ask them to guess the word. For example, you might say /p/ /e/ /t/, and they must answer with "pet." This is great for building phonemic awareness, but it will also help with blending sounds, which we'll look at in the next chapter.

17

BLENDING AND DECODING WORDS

Before we go any further here, I want to emphasize that it's important not to push this stage until your child is ready. Think back to everything we discussed about reading readiness in Chapter Four. Once we get to blending and decoding words, we're talking about reading, and there's absolutely no point in trying to force this until your little one has shown you the signs that they're ready. It will have the opposite effect to the one you're looking for: They don't have the skills in place to make a success of it, and you run the risk of removing the joy from reading.

With that said, if your child has shown you that they're ready and they have sound phonological awareness, you may find you're ready to move on to this stage before they start school. However, although they will be able to blend simple sounds to make and read words, it's worth bearing in mind that there is more than just the letter sounds they will need to know before they can completely decode language. They will also need to be familiar with a few consonant blends, digraphs, and trigraphs. We'll get to them in a moment.

BLENDING SOUNDS TO MAKE SIMPLE WORDS

Once children are secure in the sounds of the letters, they will be able to make and decode simple CVC words by blending and segmenting the units of sound they contain. When we talk about "blending" sounds, what we mean is being able to look at the word "bat" and slowly say each sound it contains: /b/ /a/ /t/. By speeding up the sounds, they blend them together to successfully read the word. Here are a few ideas for activities you can use to help your child practice blending (remember that you should only look at simple CVC words at this stage: Longer words will require more knowledge, which we'll look at shortly).

Songs: I've used *If You're Happy and You Know It* in school for teaching children to blend, and it works well at home one-on-one too. Singing is familiar to your child as they've grown up with you doing it, and it makes it a fun way to introduce blending without needing any formal teaching. Think of the original tune of the song, and switch up the words so they say:

If you recognize the word, shout it out!
If you recognize the word, shout it out!
If you recognize the word,
You can tell me what you've heard.
If you recognize the word, shout it out!

You can then give your child the sounds for a CVC word and ask them to try to blend the sounds to find the word (e.g., /d/ /o/ /g/ = "dog"). You can be as creative as you like with songs: If you can think of another song that would work, go for it!

Oral blending: Oral blending involves stretching out words so that children can hear how the sounds work together. It helps them to blend the sounds seamlessly when they come to read, rather than ending up with a choppy-sounding word with pauses between the sounds. Let's take the word, "hat." Say it to your child, stretching it out slowly: "hhaatt." Ask your child to say it in the same stretched out way, and then ask them to repeat it at a normal pace. Doing this helps them understand the relationship between the sounds and the complete word, and helps them to see how those sounds blend to create it.

Blending slide: This is another one I've used at school that translates well to the home environment. All you'll need is a picture of a slide, and some letter cards or shapes. We'll use the word "sun" as an example. Make the vowel "climb" to the top of the slide and call for help by making its sound: /u/.

Then bring the initial sound, the "s," to the top of the slide, and combine them: /su/. Place the final sound, the "n," at the bottom of the slide, and have the "s" and the "u" slide down to join them to form the full word: "sun." Have your child join in with making the sounds.

Robot talk: Another activity used in school that works well at home is to make yourself into a robot, talking in a slow, stilted robot voice: "I am a robot. Please help me. What do I see? I see /r/ /e/ /d/." Ask your child to repeat the word in robot talk, and then blend the sounds to answer your question.

Letter tiles: You can use letter tiles, magnetic letters, or letter cards to do this. It simply involves using manipulatives to blend the letter sounds and form words. Give your child the letters "b," "e" and "d," for example, and see if they can say the sounds out loud and put them together to form the word "bed."

DECODING WORDS

The next step on from being able to blend sounds is to decode a word using the same knowledge. If your child can blend the letters "m," "a," and "t," they can read the word "mat." You can consolidate this by using pictures and discussion to relate the word to its meaning. You can move on from single words to simple CVC sentences (e.g., "A cat sat on a mat.") Note that in this example, I used the word "a" instead of "the." This example can be decoded using phonetic knowledge alone. However, not all sentences can be, and to read the sentence, *"The* cat sat on *the* mat," your child will also need to recognize the sight word, "the." We'll look at sight words in the next chapter.

Discuss the meaning of the sentence with your child. Talk about the picture that accompanies it and try to relate it to your child's experiences: "Do we have a mat like that?" or "What cats do we know?" You can also consolidate their understanding further by playing games with swapping the first sound in a word: "What happens if we change the /m/ in 'mat' for a /h/? Do you think the cat would like sitting on a hat?"

A STEP BEYOND THE LETTER SOUNDS

Recognizing phonemes that are represented by more than one letter is important if a child is to get beyond reading simple CVC words. In the English language, we have several letters that work together to form unique sounds, and when we read, we need to know what these are. Decoding and blending can be taught at the same time as digraphs and consonant blends, and a child can begin blending many words before they know all of the other sounds they'll need to be a proficient reader. However, they will need this extended knowledge, and this can be built at the same time.

I don't want to overwhelm you with detail about this at this point, and as a reader yourself, you already know what these sounds are, even if you don't know the names for them. However, you'll probably run into this terminology when your child starts school, so it'll be useful to have it in your awareness now.

Consonant digraphs: A digraph is a combination of two letters which represent a single sound. Consonant digraphs are those containing only consonants. Some, like "ch," "sh," "ck," and "th" make a new sound, while others are simply different spellings of sounds—silent partners if you will (think "wh," "mb," and "wr").

Vowel digraphs: In a vowel digraph, at least one of those letters is a vowel—for example the /ea/ sound in "meat" or the /oy/ in "boy."

Trigraphs: A trigraph works on the same principle as a digraph, but instead of being made up of two letters, it has three. Good examples are the /tch/ sound in "watch" and the /igh/ sound in "sigh."

Consonant blends: Sometimes called consonant clusters, consonant blends are groups of consonants that make a distinct sound. Think of "bl" as we see in the word "black" or "sw" as we see in "sweet." These blends don't represent a single sound as a diagraph does, but they do blend together. If you were to stretch out the sounds, you would still hear the two sounds that make the whole.

TIPS FOR TEACHING BLENDS, DIGRAPHS, AND TRIGRAPHS

Firstly, rest assured that your child will be taught all these things at school, and it may be that they're not ready to tackle them before that point. I thought carefully about how to organize this chapter because it would be easy to fall into formal teaching methods. I want to avoid this here, and help you find natural and fun ways to build this kind of teaching into your home life. However, if you feel your child is ready and you want to introduce them early, here are a few tips for doing so.

Digraphs (both consonant and vowel) can be taught in the same way that single-letter phonemes are taught. Just as your child has learned that "s" makes a /s/ sound, they can learn that "sh" makes a /sh/ sound. Teaching them these, therefore, is as simple as doing all the things you did to teach them the sounds the letters of the alphabet make individually. Instead of presenting them with a single "s," however, you're going to present them with "sh."

As for blends, this moves more into blending and decoding, and it's exactly why pronouncing pure sounds without a schwa is important. As your child begins to blend sounds, they will learn that "bl" blends the /b/ and /l/ sounds. If they had learned to pronounce the /b/ sound with an /u/ at the end of it, this would be problematic.

For digraphs and trigraphs, the letter combinations can be presented as a unit. For blends, I think a kinesthetic approach is more useful so that they understand that this is two sounds coming together rather than one unique sound. For example, you might take the fridge magnet letters "b" and "l," and with one in each hand, bring them together while you demonstrate the sounds being blended.

In schools, children are usually introduced to consonant blends systematically. So, rather than teaching them all at once, perhaps the "l" blends are introduced first (think "bl," "cl," and "pl") or the "r" blends (for example, "br," "cr," and "dr").

The more multisensory you can make the process, the better. If your child can physically manipulate the letters, they have access to a deeper understanding of the way language works.

Use sand, play dough, shaving foam, or letter blocks to make the experience more interactive.

For home use, I'm a big fan of wall charts. This allows children to become familiar with seeing these combinations of letters, and makes them a friendly thing to see around them. Most charts show the blends, digraphs, or trigraphs alongside a picture, which is helpful for children contextualizing how the sound works in the word. What I would do is first introduce your child to the chart, talking about how the blends/digraphs work. Look at all the pictures and ask your child to name them, listening to the blend in the word.

You can then relate sound games to the chart. If you're using a blends chart, say a word that begins one of the blends and ask the child to find the picture on the chart that starts with the same sound. You can do the same for digraphs and trigraphs, but in these cases, you may need to look for word pictures that rhyme or have the same sound in the middle of the word.

Once children have begun to blend sounds, opportunities are everywhere! Encourage them to sound out words in environmental print; leave words on the fridge for them to decode; ask them if they can read a word in the title of their bedtime story… The world is your oyster! If you come across words that use a consonant blend or a digraph/trigraph they don't yet know, show them the sound the letters represent. Be led by your child, and remember: Don't push them before they're ready.

★ Game Time!

Simon Says: I always love an opportunity to turn a classic game into a sneaky learning opportunity! Play the game as you usually would, but instead of simply instructing your child to pat their leg, ask them to blend the words to figure out the instruction. For example, you might say, "Simon says /p/ /a/ /t/ your /l/ /e/ /g/."

18

THOSE PESKY SIGHT WORDS!

The English language is complex, and you can't decode it using phonics alone. Some words can't be sounded out, and these need to be learned. They are often confused with high-frequency words, which are decodable words that children may come across frequently before they learn the rules that govern them. However, although there are overlaps, they are not the same thing. Sight words are the words that will never be decodable, no matter what spelling rules you learn.

There's no reason to teach your child sight words before they go to school, but if they have begun to blend sounds and decode words, they should be taught that not all words can be sounded out. And if they've shown you that they're reading-ready and they have an interest, or if you wish to support them once they go to school, here's what you can do.

THE DOLCH SIGHT WORDS LIST

In 1937, Dr. Edward Dolch developed the Dolch sight word list, which included a mixture of high-frequency words and sight words. He believed that if these words were memorized, new readers would become more fluent, facing fewer stumbling blocks as they read. The list is still often used with students up to third grade, and contains 80 percent of the words you're likely to find in a children's book.

The full Dolch list is copyrighted, so I can't include it here. However, you can easily access it online by using the QR code below.

I have, however, been able to include the words usually used with kindergarten and first grade, so if you're thinking of introducing your child to sight words, these are good ones to start with.

the	one	to	my	and	me	a	big
I	come	you	blue	it	red	in	where
said	jump	for	away	up	here	look	help
is	make	go	yellow	we	two	little	play
down	run	can	find	see	three	not	funny

As you can see, some of these words will be decodable once your child has acquired enough knowledge. These are high-frequency words, and they're still worth introducing to your child if they're beginning to decode words, as they'll probably meet these words before they learn the rules associated with them.

HOW TO INTRODUCE SIGHT WORDS

The best way to familiarize your child with sight words is to introduce them early on in a natural way. Even before you explicitly teach them these words, it's helpful if they've been exposed to them. Point out sight words in the environment, reading signs in the grocery store, or pointing them out in leaflets or story books. A lot of rhyming books are helpful for this because many repeated phrases contain sight words —often "I" and "the," for example. As your child joins in with you repeating rhymes, point to the words as you go.

If your child is ready to learn some of these words, I'd recommend taking a multisensory approach. Get them to fill in missing letters or reorder them to form a sight word. You can also get them to practice writing the word in the air with their finger (you'll need to have the word displayed somewhere so they can see it). Encourage them to use the whole arm for this, as it engages more muscles and thus leaves a greater imprint on their memory.

Give them opportunities to interact with sight words at home, whether that's through displaying them on the fridge, including them in games, or making them part of art projects.

One final useful tip I have for you is to play categorizing games with your child. Write down a mixture of sight words and decodable words on cards, and work with your child to sort them into categories. Which ones can they sound out, and which ones break the rules? Your child is not ready for this activity, however, until they can confidently sound out words.

Sight Word Activity Ideas

Shaving cream: Fill a tray with shaving cream, and write a sight word (that your child is already familiar with) in the foam. Can they read it? Let them copy it in the shaving foam and erase it ready for the next word: You want the activity to be as interactive as possible.

Train track sentences: If you have Brio or some other train-track building activity at home, this presents you with a great opportunity for teaching sight words. Write single words on labels that together create a whole sentence, using a mixture of decodable words and the sight word you want your child to practice—for example, "The man went to the shop" (Note: this particular example includes a consonant blend (nt) and a digraph (sh)—make sure that whatever sentence you use is compatible with your child's reading ability). Stick each label on a separate piece of train track, jumble them up, and ask your child to build a railway that makes a whole sentence. As well as working on sight words, this will give your child valuable sentence-building practice.

Magic reveal: Write sight words on a piece of thick paper in white crayon. Ask your child to paint over the paper in watercolor paints. As they do this, the word will be revealed. Ask them to tell you what word they've discovered.

Egg hunt: Collect plastic eggs (the kind you open to find a toy). When you have a good collection, write sight words on strips of paper and hide them in the eggs. Then hide the eggs around your home or backyard, and go on an egg hunt with your child. For every egg they find, ask them to tell you what word is hiding inside.

Bingo: Bingo comes in handy for everything! Create Bingo boards including a mixture of decodable words and any sight word you may be working on with your child. Call out the words, and let them mark them off as they find them.

Word walk: You'll need a bit of space for this one. Write down a mixture of decodable words and sight words on large pieces of card or paper, and lay them out in a path around your home. Your child must follow the path, reading the words as they go.

The trick with introducing sight words to your child is not to introduce too many at once, and to make it as fun and interactive as you can. Any way you can make it into a game is great. In fact, the game below is a firm favorite in our house. My older two love to play *Catch the Word* with their little sister. It's great bonding time for them, and she loves learning from her older siblings.

★ Game Time!

Catch the Word: Label ten small balls with a sight word, or use a mixture of decodable words and sight words. Play catch with your child using different balls, having them read the word on the ball with each catch.

19

NOW IT'S THEIR TURN TO READ TO YOU...

One of the first things we looked at was the importance of reading to your child, but once they begin to read themselves, it's equally as important to hear them read to you. There should be no pressure to do this before they're ready, but even before they're actually reading, this process can be set up very early on through interactive story time. This way, you'll find it much easier to naturally segue into sessions in which your child reads to you.

TIPS FOR LISTENING TO YOUR CHILD READ

You'll need books aimed at your child's reading level. Bear in mind that these are likely to be more simple than the books you're reading to them—remember that their listening age is usually higher than their reading age. Choose a quiet time when distractions are at a minimum, and give your child your full attention as they read. If they struggle with a word, first, give them the opportunity to self-correct. Then encourage them to skip it and read the rest of the sentence. Then ask them to return to the word: "What word would make sense in that place?" Remind them what they know about letter sounds, and if they still can't decode the word, give them the right one and let them continue. Praise them often, and be careful not to dwell on mistakes. It's a lot like when they're little and you're modeling the correct pronunciation of a word: Focus on supplying them with the right one rather than drawing attention to the error.

Keep in mind the comprehension-building strategies you've been working on until this point. Continue to talk about the book: the characters; the pictures; how the story might end; what might happen next. Relate what they're reading to their everyday experiences to help them consolidate their understanding and build new schemas.

In my opinion, reading to your kids and hearing them read to you should be an ongoing part of their childhood, and if you've been doing the first one, you should find that the second follows naturally. I hear each of my children read after school, and we keep this as a separate event from story time, which I still do before they go to bed.

★ Game Time!

Remake a Picture Book: Okay, so it's not really a game, but it's a fun activity that children will love. I've included this one here because it relates to the understanding of the whole story, but it is a pre-reading activity that can be done before your child is reading ready. Get hold of a second-hand copy of a picture book your child is familiar with and remove the pages. Ask your child to build the story back in the right order. See if they can retell the story in their own words, paving the way for reading to you later.

PART III

GOING FORWARD

20

THE PARENT PITFALLS YOU CAN EASILY AVOID

As long as you remain positive and don't put too much pressure on your child, all the language and literacy support you give them is valuable. I don't, therefore, want to spend too long on what *not* to do. However, I do recognize that parents worry about getting things wrong, so I've compiled a list of common mistakes so you can be confident that you're not making any.

Telling rather than asking: It's tempting to tell your child what a book will be about before they start reading it to you, but a better strategy is to ask your child to predict what the story will be about based on the clues the book gives them. This is true both for a book you're reading to them and a book they're reading to you. Make reading time interactive, and use discussion to build their comprehension skills.

Asking too many questions: While questioning is important to building their comprehension skills, you want to be careful not to interrogate them. A good strategy for avoiding this is to frame your questions as comments instead. Make a comment about the point you want them to talk about, and encourage them to complete your thought.

Skipping rereading: Don't be tempted to think that once you've read a book with your child once, there's no point in revisiting it. The more times they engage with a book, the more familiar they'll become with it, and this will build confidence and comprehension.

Pitching it too high: I've come across parents so eager to read a childhood favorite of their own with their little one that they jump in too quickly. While their listening age will be greater than their reading age for a while, they won't be ready for complex plots and character arcs that early. Children's books are written with age in mind, and are designed to keep them interested in the story, as well as using language they can access easily. It's fine for a story to include a few complex words you'll need to explain to your child, but they'll need to be able to understand the content themselves in order to build up a love of reading. Save those childhood classics for later—you'll have a much higher chance of success.

Correcting every error: If your child is the one doing the reading, try to avoid the temptation to correct every mistake. Keep in mind the ones they tend to struggle with, and come back to them later. If you have to stop their reading too often, they'll struggle with engagement and comprehension, and this may harm their relationship with reading.

Putting the book down quickly: We've all been there: You're busy; dinner needs cooking; and your eldest needs driving to soccer practice. Try to avoid the temptation to put the book down as soon as you've finished reading. Factor in time to spend a few minutes discussing the story afterward. This encourages children to look at the whole experience of reading, and helps you to nurture comprehension and deeper level thinking skills.

Not giving characters voices: I don't want you to feel intimidated by the idea that every story should be a performance. However, it will help your child's understanding and engagement if you're able to read expressively and change your tone to fit the characters' feelings.

Ignoring illustrations: The illustrations are part of the text, and they contain clues to help your child understand the story. Encourage them to explore the story by discussing the pictures, thus making reading an immersive experience.

Interrupting them: Whether it's you or your child doing the reading, try to let the process flow without too many interruptions. While you do want to check their understanding here and there, it's important not to stop the story too much. Doing so will make it harder to access, and will make the reading experience less fun for them.

Reading alternate lines: I've seen some parents take the approach of reading a line of a story to their child and then asking them to read the next one. The problem with this is that it doesn't allow them to practice sustained reading, and it also interrupts the flow of the story, which can affect comprehension. There's nothing wrong with sharing the reading, but if you do this, read a whole page, and then ask them to reread it. If, however, you notice that this approach seems to bore them, stop immediately. You don't want reading to become a chore.

Teaching letter sounds in alphabetical order: We looked at the order in which to introduce letter sounds in Chapter Fourteen. Teaching the letter sounds in alphabetical order will slow their progress, so revisit this chapter to double-check.

Using only capital letters: It's important for children to know the capital letters, but be wary of overusing toys and resources that feature them. Most of the text they will encounter will be in lower case. Capital letters are often more commonly seen in toys and games because they're cheaper to produce, but relying on them won't help your child's reading.

Ignoring natural reading progression: As we've seen, reading is composed of skills that are best built up in a sequential order. This allows for a strong foundation and aligns with the way children are taught at school. Follow the order we've discussed for the best results.

Pushing them before they're ready: This is, perhaps, the most critical mistake to avoid. If you push your child to read before they're ready, they'll quickly become frustrated, and it will be difficult to nurture a love of reading. When children come to associate reading with boredom and frustration at a young age, this can be very hard to undo later. Rest assured, your child *will* be ready to learn to read. Just let them get there in their own time.

I haven't included this chapter in order to scare you. You're going to be absolutely fine, and if you don't pressure them or push them before they're ready, you're not going to put them off reading or hinder their progress. However, in order to nurture their confidence and instill in them a love of reading, be aware of the mistakes other parents have made, and try to avoid making them yourself.

21

SUPPORTING A LOVE OF READING FROM THIS DAY FORTH

Once your child goes to school, they'll be building on everything they've learned at home, and you'll want to find ways you can support them without contradicting anything they're learning during the day. The good news is that this is basically just a question of continuing to do what you've already been doing from the beginning of your child's reading journey.

Continue to read to them (every day if possible), even once they're able to read to themselves. This will allow them to access material beyond their reading level, give them new challenges, and give you a chance for that all-important bonding time. Listen to them read every day, and continue to talk about environmental print. There are always interesting things to talk about in the language we see around us every day, even once your child is reading independently.

Continue to keep the conversation flowing at home, and use every opportunity for conversation.

FUN ACTIVITIES FOR SUPPORTING READING

Art: The majority of children love drawing and coloring, and you can use this natural interest to help them support their literacy skills. Ask your child to illustrate their favorite part of a book they've recently read, or draw their favorite character. This provides an excellent opportunity for discussion, and it also helps your child to focus on different aspects of a story and develop their comprehension skills.

Shopping: I'm all for building literacy into everyday experiences, and shopping is a great one. When you're making your grocery list, ask your child to write the items down as you list them. When you get to the store, ask them to read the items out so you can find them.

Cooking: Show me a child who doesn't love baking—even if it's just so they can eat the results! Look at the recipe with your child, discussing how recipes are arranged and how to follow them. Depending on their reading level, they can read out the ingredients or instructions, or you can read each step to them, encouraging them to follow the steps in order.

Make a dictionary: A dictionary can be an empowering tool, especially when it's made by your child and contains the words they find particularly challenging. Make a booklet or give them a fresh notebook, and ask them to write a word they've recently learned at the top of each page. They can then look for pictures in magazines, or draw an illustration of the word to help consolidate their understanding. Beneath this, they can either write down the meaning of the word or a sentence containing that word. This process will not only help them to practice the word; it will also help them to understand its meaning.

Journaling: Encourage your child to start a journal. Make sure they understand its purpose before they begin, and discuss the kinds of things they might want to include (e.g., what happened at school, meeting a new friend, or how they felt about a particular event). Liam and Amelia both do a version of this, and I think that part of the reason they're compelled to is that I also keep a journal. Remember how powerful the behavior you model to them is.

Make a bookmark: While making a bookmark doesn't directly relate to your child's reading skills, it does give them a sense of ownership of their reading journey. It also builds the idea of reading into everyday life, and helps them to think of it as an important practice. If you do want to make it a more literacy-based activity, ask your child to write details about the book they're reading on the back of the bookmark. This might include the title, author, publisher, and publication date, giving them a complete picture of what's involved in producing a book.

I have seen with my older children that these strategies work: Both of them love reading—and my little one is well on her way to joining them. I'm certain that living in a book-rich environment and being a family who reads is central to this. We now have whole-family story time on a Sunday too. We're currently working our way through the *Harry Potter* series. Sometimes I read; sometimes my husband does; and sometimes Liam takes charge. It was a friend who suggested this to me, and I have to say, it's my favorite time of the week.

22

READING GLOSSARY

I wanted to include this chapter because I know I've used some technical vocabulary throughout the book, and your exposure to this is only going to grow once your child starts school. However, your children don't need to know these words, and it's not crucial that you do either. This isn't by any means an exhaustive list; I've simply included some of the words you're most likely to come across on your child's reading journey so that you don't feel lost at those parent-teacher conferences. Terms I've already defined explicitly have been left out.

Accuracy: When accuracy is mentioned in relation to reading, it simply refers to the child's ability to recognize words accurately.

Affixes: Affixes are the parts of words attached to the beginnings (prefixes) or ends (suffixes) of words—e.g., **un**happy (un- is the prefix); thank**ful** (-ful) is the suffix.

Aligned materials: You may come across this phrase in literature sent home from your child's school. It simply refers to the materials used to reinforce teaching, and may include activities, texts, or manipulatives.

Alliteration: This is when the first sound in a word is repeated within a text (e.g., The **b**right **b**lue **b**all **b**ounced on the **b**each.)

Antonym: A word with the opposite meaning of a given word (e.g., "sad" is an antonym for "happy").

Automaticity: This refers to any complex behavior that can be executed without conscious awareness. In relation to reading, it is used when children are able to recognize words automatically rather than needing to decode them.

Base words: These are the words from which others are formed. (e.g., "care" is the base word for "cares," "cared," "careless," "caring," "careful," and "carefully.") You may sometimes hear these called "free morphemes."

Bloom's taxonomy: This is something you may see referred to in literature from your child's school, and is a framework for categorizing different types of questioning commonly used in schools. It includes knowledge, comprehension, application, analysis, synthesis, and evaluation.

Chunked text: If your child's text has been separated into phrases with slash marks, this is chunking, and its purpose is to help children practice reading phrases with fluency.

Chunking: This is a decoding strategy that breaks words into more manageable chunks (e.g., /happ/i/ness). You could also come across this word in relation to chunked text.

Comprehension strategies: These are the techniques used for teaching reading comprehension. They include summarizing, predicting, and inferring meaning from context.

Context clues: These are the clues in sentences, whole texts, pictures, or examples that readers can use to help them work out the meanings of unfamiliar words.

Cooperative learning: This is when students work together in pairs or small groups, and is commonly used for teaching comprehension strategies.

Decodable text: This is text in which the majority of words are made up of letter sounds that have already been taught. Schools use it to help children practice particular decoding skills and pave the way for applying their knowledge to independent reading.

Diphthong: This is a vowel sound which is formed by the tongue changing position part way through. Often these vowel sounds feel as though they have two separate parts (e.g., /ow/ and /oy/).

Direct vocabulary teaching: This is designed to teach important and difficult words in order to aid reading comprehension when children come across them in a text.

Dyslexia: This is a specific learning difficulty that affects written and oral language.

Emergent literacy: This refers to the pre-reading skills children must develop before they are able to read and write.

Etymology: This refers to the historical development of a word's meaning from its origin. The majority of words in the English language have their roots in Latin or Greek.

Fluency: This refers to a child's ability to read a text quickly, with accuracy, good expression, and sound comprehension.

Grapheme: This is a letter or combination of letters that represents a single sound. It may be made up of between one and four letters.

Graphic and semantic organizers: These are visual frameworks designed to organize the main points of a text. They allow children to see the internal processes required for comprehension, thus boosting their understanding.

High-frequency words: There are between 300 and 500 words that make up a large proportion of the words we see in print, and automatic recognition is necessary for fluent reading.

Homograph: Homographs are words with the same spelling but different meanings (e.g., "bat," which can either be an animal or a piece of sporting equipment).

Homonym: Homonyms are words with the same sound but a different spelling (e.g., "knight" and "night").

Homophone: Homophones are words with the same pronunciation that may or may not be spelled in the same way. They have different meanings (e.g., "sea" and "see" or "lie" to mean "in a horizontal position," or "to be untruthful").

Indirect vocabulary learning: This is when children learn the meanings of words through hearing or seeing them in different contexts.

Intervention program: This is a form of teaching designed to meet a child's individual learning needs in a particular area. It is used to provide targeted intervention for individuals or small groups who are struggling with reading.

Metacognition: This is having an awareness of your own thought process, and for children, that means being able to consciously think about their reading or learning while they're doing it.

Monitoring comprehension: This allows readers to know whether they understand what they're reading or not, and involves being able to use the appropriate strategy for fixing any issues.

Morpheme: This is the smallest unit of meaning in a word. It may be a whole word, or it could be part of a word (e.g., in "thoughtless," there are two morphemes: "thought" and "less").

Orthographic mapping: This refers to the ability to recognize sight words accurately and effortlessly.

Phoneme: This is the smallest unit of sound in a word that has an effect on meaning (e.g., if the first phoneme in "dog" is changed from /d/ to /l/, the word becomes "log").

Phoneme manipulation: This is the act of adding, deleting, or substituting phonemes in a word to create new words.

Phonemic awareness: This refers to the ability to recognize and manipulate the sounds in speech (e.g., being able to blend the sounds /b/ /a/ /g/ to say the word "bag").

Phonics: This is a method of teaching reading that focuses on the relationship between spoken sounds and written letters (the alphabetic principle). There are a few different ways phonics is taught:

- **Analogy-based phonics** (Children are taught to decode words they don't know by using parts of words they do know.)
- **Analytic phonics** (Children are taught to analyze the relationships between sounds and letters in words they've already learned. Sounds are not pronounced in isolation.)

- **Embedded phonics** (Children are taught letter-sound relationships as part of sight word reading. This is usually used when a child is having difficulty with reading a particular word.)
- **Synthetic phonics** (Children are taught how to translate letters or combinations of letters into sounds and blend them to make words.)

Phonological awareness: This is when we understand that spoken words are composed of individual sounds, and includes everything from word awareness to rhyme recognition and phonemic awareness.

Pragmatics: This refers to making the appropriate word choice for the context in order to ensure effective communication.

Prosody: This refers to the ability to read with expression and correct intonation. It is part of being a fluent reader.

Reciprocal teaching: This is a multistrategy approach to teaching comprehension in schools, focusing on four key strategies: asking questions, summarizing, clarifying, and predicting.

Schema: A schema is the prior knowledge and experience that we bring to a text.

Semantics: This refers to the way meaning is conveyed through language.

Shwa: This is the vowel sound (usually /u/) we can hear in an unstressed syllable (e.g., the "a" in "balloon").

Sight words: These are often irregular or high-frequency words, but any word that can be recognized automatically counts as a sight word.

Summarizing: This refers to being able to reduce a text to its main point or key ideas. It's a skill taught in order to help children generate and connect ideas, remove unnecessary points, and retain important information.

Syllable: This is part of a word that contains just one vowel sound (e.g., "sun-shine").

Vocabulary: Vocabulary involves both the pronunciation and meaning of words.

CONCLUSION

I think the fact that you want your child to love reading and take ownership of their learning journey is the biggest step you can take in helping them to become confident and fluent readers. If I could give you only one piece of advice, I'd say this: Don't teach your child to read. And by this, of course, I don't mean you shouldn't do any of the things we've discussed in our time together. I mean don't give them formal lessons at home. Don't push them before they're ready. Instead, be led by their development and interest, and let them show you they're ready to read in their own time. Show them that reading is fun. Help them to access the language all around them. Spend time together, enjoying conversation and song, and make reading a part of your daily life. Do this, and I promise you, the rest will follow.

Giving your child the skills they need to become engaged and fluent readers doesn't require a single formal lesson before they start school. Everything we've talked about here can be built into daily life, and you can start now. Remember how successful the Finnish model is? The key to that is allowing those emerging literacy skills to develop through play, creativity, and lots of exposure to language. Look for every opportunity you can to engage your child in sounds, words, and print: You're at the beginning of an exciting adventure.

If you were feeling overwhelmed at the start of this journey, I promise you, you're not alone. I've lost track of the number of parents I've spoken to who have worried about how they can help their child to read and give them the best start they can. But we can help those parents out. If they can easily find the resources they need that show them how easy it is to have a huge impact on their child's reading development, I just know we can ease a lot of minds. And how can we do that? Well, you could start by **leaving a review of this book on Amazon**. That, after all, is how people find the resources they need. And ultimately, that is how we'll help more children to thrive in the wonderful world of reading.

Scan the QR code below to leave a review!

freeguide.blueyonderpublications.com

REFERENCES

Allied Health, Speech, Language, Hearing and Audiology, Alberta Health Services. (2021, February 1). *Phonological awareness: Learning the sounds in words*. MyHealth.Alberta.ca. https://myhealth.alberta.ca/speech-language-hearing/language/for-preschoolers/phonological-awareness-learning-sounds-in-words

All 220 Dolch words by grade in frequency order. (n.d.). Dolch Word. https://www.dolchword.net/printables/All220DolchWordsByGradeFreq.pdf

Biba, J. (2019, October 24). *5 ways to make learning sight words easier for your kids*. Scholastic. https://www.scholastic.com/parents/books-and-reading/raise-a-reader-blog/sight-words-activities-books.html

Blending and segmenting games. (2019, December 26). Reading Rockets. https://www.readingrockets.org/strategies/blending_games

Borkowsky, F. (2016, October 6). *Literacy: Finland vs. USA.* High Five Literacy and Academic Coaching. https://highfiveliteracy.com/2016/10/06/literacy-finland-vs-usa/

Brainspring. (2020, July 30). *5 ways to practice phonemic awareness at home.* Orton-Gillingham Weekly. https://brainspring.com/ortongillinghamweekly/5-ways-practice-phonemic-awareness-home/

Burns, T. (2019, March 14). *Bedtime story prompts for parents who can't think of any stories to tell.* Brightly. https://www.readbrightly.com/bedtime-story-prompts-for-parents/

Caine, J. (2016, January 3). *Teaching consonant blends, digraphs, and trigraphs.* Pearson. https://longmanhomeusa.com/blog/teaching-consonant-blends-digraphs-and-trigraphs/

Chen, G. (n.d.). *"What happens next?": Strategies for teaching your child sequencing skills.* Stage Learning. https://blog.stageslearning.com/blog/what-happens-next-strategies-for-teaching-your-child-sequencing-skills

Children's Book Council. (2013, November 7). *Choosing a*

child's book. Reading Rockets. https://www.readingrockets.org/article/choosing-childs-book

Cooper, S. (2021, August 21). *12 favorite rhyming books for preschoolers*. Teaching 2 and 3 Year Olds. https://teaching2and3yearolds.com/favorite-rhyming-books-for-preschoolers/

Crean, M. (2016, September 18). *6 helpful activities to teach the skill of blending*. Top Notch Teaching. https://topnotchteaching.com/lesson-ideas/blending/

Crean, M. (2020, March 3). *4 useful strategies to improve phoneme manipulation*. Top Notch Teaching. https://topnotchteaching.com/lesson-ideas/phoneme-manipulation/

Diaz, V. (2018, March 29). *50 must-read board books for babies*. Book Riot. https://bookriot.com/board-books-for-babies/

Duursma, E., Augustyn, M., & Zuckerman, B. (2008, August). Reading aloud to children: The evidence. *Archives of Disease in Childhood, 93*(7), 554–557. https://doi.org/10.1136/adc.2006.106336

8 easy ways to teach sight words to preschoolers. (2020, July 17). ABCDee Learning. https://abcdeelearning.com/how-to-teach-sight-words/

Environmental print. (2019, December 30). Reading Rockets. https://www.readingrockets.org/article/environmental-print

Erickson, J. (n.d.). *5 common mistakes parents make when teaching reading.* The Unlikely Homeschool. https://www.theunlikelyhomeschool.com/2020/06/early-reading-skills.html

Greenberg, J., & Koohi, A. L. (n.d.). *How to build language and literacy through powerful conversations.* The Hanen Centre. https://www.hanen.org/Helpful-Info/Articles/How-to-Build-Language-and-Literacy-Through-Powerfu.aspx

Halliday, N. (n.d.). *What are digraphs and how to teach them.* You Clever Monkey. https://www.youclevermonkey.com/2016/07/teaching-digraphs.html

Jordan, B. (2021, March 11). *How to teach vowels.* Mama Teaches. https://mamateaches.com/how-to-teach-vowels/

Jenna. (2020, September 6). *Proven order to teach letters that will get your child reading faster!* Simply Working Mama. https://www.simplyworkingmama.com/order-to-teach-letters/

Jensen, K. (2021, April 19). *The best children's books by age: A guide to great reading.* Book Riot. https://bookriot.com/best-childrens-books-by-age/

Koralek, D., & Collins, R. (2013, November 7). *How most children learn to read.* Reading Rockets. https://www.readingrockets.org/article/how-most-children-learn-read

Kuppen, S. (2018, November 15). *Rhymes in early childhood.* BookTrust. https://www.booktrust.org.uk/news-and-features/features/2018/november/rhymes-in-early-childhood/

Language development in children: 0–8 years. (2021, February 17). Raising Children Network. https://raisingchildren.net.au/babies/development/language-development/language-development-0-8

Levin, V. (2010, January 16). *Environmental print ideas, activities, games and more!* Pre-K Pages. https://www.pre-kpages.com/environmental_print/

Logan, J., Justice, L., Yumuş, M., & Chaparro-Moreno, L. (2019). When Children Are Not Read to at Home: The Million Word Gap. *Journal Of Developmental & Behavioral Pediatrics, 40*(5), 383-386. doi: 10.1097/dbp.0000000000000657.

Marcin, A. (2020, October 14). *Reading to children: Why it's so important and how to start.* Healthline. https://www.healthline.com/health/childrens-health/reading-to-children

Mattiessen, C. (2019, April 7). *Top 5 parenting fears and what you can do about them.* BabyCenter. https://www.babycenter.com/family/motherhood/top-5-parenting-fears-and-what-you-can-do-about-them_3656609

Mcilroy, T. (2021, June 11). *10 ideas for developing pre-reading skills.* Empowered Parents. https://empoweredparents.co/10-ideas-developing-pre-reading-spelling-skills/

Mcilroy, T. (2021, August 24). *Pre-writing activities every parent should do with their preschooler at home.* Empowered Parents. https://empoweredparents.co/pre-writing-activities/

Mcilroy, T. (2021, November 22). *12 critical thinking activities for kids.* Empowered Parents. https://empoweredparents.co/how-to-develop-your-childs-thinking-skills-during-storytime/

Mendelsohn, A. L., & Klass, P. (2018). Early language exposure and middle school language and IQ: Implications for primary prevention. *Pediatrics, 142*(4). https://doi.org/10.1542/peds.2018-2234

Merga, M. K., Gardner, P., Roni, S. M., & Ledger, S. (2018, April 1). *Five tips to help you make the most of reading to your children.* The Conversation. https://theconversation.com/five-tips-to-help-you-make-the-most-of-reading-to-your-children-93659

Morin, A. (2019, August 5). *Reading skills at different ages.* Understood. https://www.understood.org/articles/en/reading-skills-what-to-expect-at-different-ages

Morin, A. (2020, May 18). *8 activities to encourage pre-reading and early literacy.* Verywell Family. https://www.verywellfamily.com/activities-to-encourage-pre-reading-621060

Mulvahill, E. (2021, May 7). *What are sight words?* We Are Teachers. https://www.weareteachers.com/what-are-sight-words/

Myers, R. (2019, July 23). *Look who's talking! All about child language development.* Child Development Institute. https://childdevelopmentinfo.com/child-development/language_development/#gs.j57szn

National Institutes of Health. (2017, August 24). *Speech and language developmental milestones.* Reading Rockets. https://www.readingrockets.org/article/speech-and-language-developmental-milestones

Nursery rhymes: Not just for babies! (2017, August 23). Reading Rockets. https://www.readingrockets.org/article/nursery-rhymes-not-just-babies

Ohio State University. (2019, April 4). *A "million word gap" for children who aren't read to at home.* ScienceDaily. https://www.sciencedaily.com/releases/2019/04/190404074947.htm

Osewalt, G. (2019, August 6). *7 tips to help kids understand what they read.* Understood. https://www.understood.org/articles/en/7-tips-to-help-kids-understand-what-they-read

Phonological (sound) awareness. (2016, November 27). Kid Sense. https://childdevelopment.com.au/areas-of-concern/literacy/phonological-awareness/

Phonological and phonemic awareness: In practice. (2021, June 1). Reading Rockets. https://www.readingrockets.org/teaching/reading101-course/modules/phonological-and-phonemic-awareness/phonological-and-phonemic-1

Pre-writing shapes—What are they and how to teach them? (2021, February 22). Griffin Occupational Therapy. https://www.griffinot.com/pre-writing-shapes-what-are-they-and-how-to-teach-them/

Punkoney, S. (2021, February 15). *14 things you should know about reading readiness*. The Kindergarten Connection. https://thekindergartenconnection.com/14-things-you-should-know-about-reading-readiness/

Questions to ask your child during reading. (2019, April 2). Growing Young Minds. https://gyminds.co.uk/questions-to-ask-your-child-during-reading/

Rainforest Learning Centre. (2020, October 12). *5 easy ways to teach the alphabet to preschoolers*. https://rainforestlearningcentre.ca/5-easy-ways-to-teach-the-alphabet-to-preschoolers/

Reading glossary. (2021, April 28). Reading Rockets. https://www.readingrockets.org/teaching/glossary

Reading wars: Phonics vs. whole language instruction. (n.d.). Reading Horizons. https://www.readinghorizons.com/reading-strategies/teaching/phonics-instruction/reading-wars-phonics-vs-whole-language-reading-instruction

Rhymes, rhythm and repetition. (2020, October 30). Early Childhood Education and Care. https://earlychildhood.qld.gov.au/early-years/activities-and-resources/resources-parents/read-and-count/rhymes-rhythm-and-repetition

Richards, V. (2019, February 1). *"Tell us a bedtime story!": 7 easy tips on how to make one for your kids.* HuffPost UK. https://www.huffingtonpost.co.uk/entry/tell-us-a-story-seven-easy-tips-on-how-to-make-up-a-bedtime-story-for-your-kids_uk_5c5418c9e4b01d3c1f12643d

Schwartz, S., & Sparks, S. (2019, October 2). *How do kids learn to read? What the science says.* Education Week. https://www.edweek.org/teaching-learning/how-do-kids-learn-to-read-what-the-science-says/2019/10

Seymour, K. (2017, January 23). *Schema theory and reading comprehension.* WeHaveKids. https://wehavekids.com/education/Reading-Comprehension-Theory

Sowdon, L. (2020, September 28). *Identifying 10 signs of reading readiness.* Five Senses Literature Lessons. https://www.5sensesll.com/index.php/2018/10/03/identifying-10-signs-of-reading-readiness/

Spence, B. (2019, March 12). *Free blends and digraphs chart.* This Reading Mama. https://thisreadingmama.com/free-blends-and-digraphs-chart/

Supporting language and literacy skills from 12–24 months. (n.d.). ZERO TO THREE. https://www.zerotothree.org/resources/1285-supporting-language-and-literacy-skills-from-12-24-months

Tan, R. (2018, June 23). *10 mistakes to avoid when teaching kids how to read.* https://smiletutor.sg/10-mistakes-to-avoid-when-teaching-kids-how-to-read/. https://smiletutor.sg/10-mistakes-to-avoid-when-teaching-kids-how-to-read/

Teaching letter sounds: 5 fun and easy tips. (2021, July 22). HOMER Blog. https://www.learnwithhomer.com/homer-blog/3719/letter-sounds/

10 clever games to help your child learn sight words. (2017, March 3). Curious World. https://www.curiousworld.com/blog/sight-word-games

Texas Education Agency. (2018, November 14). *The alphabetic principle.* Reading Rockets. https://www.readingrockets.org/article/alphabetic-principle

Texas Education Agency. (2019, March 1). *Key comprehension strategies to teach.* Reading Rockets. https://www.readingrockets.org/article/key-comprehension-strategies-teach

Top mistakes parents make in teaching reading to children. (2019, January 3). Reading Kingdom Blog. https://www.readingkingdom.com/blog/mistakes-parents-make-teaching-reading-children/?doing_wp_cron=1637850522.5251269340515136718750

Trouble sequencing: Why some kids do things out of order. (2019, August 5). Understood. https://www.understood.org/articles/en/trouble-with-sequencing-what-you-need-to-know

Ullery, S. (2019, September 20). *20 must-read books for first graders and second graders.* Book Riot. https://bookriot.com/books-for-first-graders-and-second/

US Department of Education. (2019, September 25). *25 activities for reading and writing fun.* Reading Rockets. https://www.readingrockets.org/article/25-activities-reading-and-writing-fun

Why rhymes and songs are so important for early years. (2019, October 18). Yellow Door. https://www.yellow-door.net/blog/the-wonder-of-rhyme/

Wierschem, J. (2018, April 2). *Scarborough's Reading Rope: A groundbreaking infographic.* International Dyslexia Association. https://dyslexiaida.org/scarboroughs-reading-rope-a-groundbreaking-infographic/

Willoughby, K. (2018, July 25). *50 must-read preschool books for little readers.* Book Riot. https://bookriot.com/must-read-preschool-books/

Wise, R. (2016, April 26). *Try these 10 fun phonics activities to teach letter sounds to children.* Education and Behavior. https://educationandbehavior.com/fun-ways-to-teach-letter-sounds/

www.ingramcontent.com/pod-product-compliance
Lightning Source LLC
Chambersburg PA
CBHW030259100526
44590CB00012B/447